Discover!
Social Studies

6

GRADE 6
Social Studies

Discover! Social Studies Instructor Guide

Published in Catasauqua, Pennsylvania by Discover Press, a division of Edovate Learning Corp.

334 2nd Street

Catasauqua, PA 18032

edovate.com

ISBN: 978-1-956330-17-5

Printed in United States of America

1st Edition

Lesson Objectives

By the end of this lesson, your student will be able to:

- explain that archaeologists uncover artifacts that tell them about ancient civilizations and cultures
- analyze images of various events in the ancient world
- identify common themes in world history
- identify the themes of geography in the study of world history

Supporting Your Student

Explore

Since this activity is about culture, your student should find items and objects in their house that have a tag or label on them that shows where they were made. You may want to help your student find objects that have this tag or label. Some ideas would be china dishes, toys, figurines, clothing, and souvenirs. To enrich this activity, have your student sort items by where they were made. They could group items from the same country or continent together.

Read

Because your student will be reading about several different themes that are closely related, it might be difficult to keep them apart. A graphic organizer to keep track of the themes might be helpful. Consider keeping a chart with the name of the theme and a symbol to help the student remember the theme. An example of the theme might be useful for the student when it is time for them to do the Practice activity. For example, your student might draw a picture of a person and Earth to remember human-environment interaction. Then they might list a dam as an example.

Practice

A discussion with the student may be helpful prior to this practice activity. For each common theme in world history, discuss modern-day examples that relate to your student's life as shown below.

- Geography: Describe the mountains, location, places, region, and rivers in your area.
- Human-Environment Interaction: Choose one of the landforms or bodies of water discussed from

the geography theme and discuss how people there would use that landform or body of water for their benefit.

- Rise of Civilizations: What city today has grown a lot? Which city in your country is the biggest? What caused it to grow so large?
- Growth and Change in Societies: Based on the discussion from Rise of Civilizations, discuss what changes would take place in that city because the population grew so large.
- Development of Political Institutions and Ideas: What type of government does the city or country currently have?
- Belief Systems: What religions do people practice today? What do they do to practice their religions?
- Interconnectedness of Societies: What state or country is near the country where the student lives? How do the countries, states, or cities work together?

Refer back to examples you discussed as your student completes the activity. For example, if they are trying to determine if a picture shows the theme of belief systems, say, "We talked about the religions people practice today and how they practice them. Does this picture show people practicing a religion?"

Learning Styles

Auditory learners may enjoy listening to recordings of ancient Greek and Roman orators who formed the foundation of democracy, which relates to the theme Development of Political Institutions and Ideas.

Visual learners may enjoy finding images of ancient civilizations and creating a collage to illustrate one of the themes of world history.

Kinesthetic learners may enjoy recreating a model of an artifact from a civilization using art and craft supplies.

Extension Activities

Replica of a Civilization

Have your student create a model of the civilization that was chosen for the Online Connection activity by using art and craft supplies or drawing a picture of what the civilization looked like. The buildings, land use, and important landmarks and bodies of water should be included. These elements will help your student describe the culture and way of life in this civilization.

Infographic of Themes

Your student can create an infographic of common themes in world history. An infographic uses visual representations like pictures, images, and charts to show and organize information on a topic. Besides drawing pictures and writing the meaning of each theme, your student may also provide examples from history that might fit into those themes. For instance, your student could include different pictures and examples that reference different political institutions or ideas including dictators, kings and queens, and democracy.

Answer Key

Explore *(Sidebar)*

Answer will vary. Possible answer: Archaeologists make a grid when digging for artifacts so they can organize the area they are working in. They can check off which areas they have searched. They can also map where they found artifacts and which artifacts were found near each other. This could give them clues about what the artifact is and how it was used. For example, if a flat shard of clay was found next to an ancient fork-like object, this might suggest it was part of a bowl or plate because both items would be used for eating.

Write *(If you were an archaeologist, what types of artifacts would you want to find or be interested in studying?)*

Answer will vary. Possible answer: I would want to study artifacts from ancient China. I would like to study artifacts that tell about daily life in Sumer.

Write *(Think about where you live. Choose one theme of geography. Use this theme to describe where you live.)*

Answers will vary depending on the place and location where your student lives. Possible answer:

1. Location: Knoxville, TN
2. Place: The place is an area near the Smoky Mountains.
3. Human-Environment Interaction: People hike to the Smoky Mountains and raft down the nearby rivers. There are many landforms and bodies of water including the Tennessee River and the Smoky Mountains.
4. Movement: People move to where I live because they can live near the mountains and because of farming and jobs.
5. Regions: I live in the southern region of the United States.

Practice

Answers may vary. Possible answers:

1. The theme is Belief Systems because the Native American tribes worshiped spirits in nature.
2. The theme is Geography (Movement) because these people are moving from place to place instead of settling into a civilization. It is also the Rise of Civilizations because it talks about how people organized themselves into communities, and it is Human-Environment Interaction because it talks about population movement to find food.
3. The theme is Interconnectedness of Societies because the Phoenicians rely on others in the area for things they need to survive. In return, the Phoenicians made ships for other societies. It is also the theme of Rise of Civilizations which looks at the rise of trade networks. Finally, it is Geography (Movement) because it deals with the exchange of ideas, materials, and physical systems between people around the world.

Answer Key

1. The theme is Human-Environment Interaction because the people in the village relied on the river to grow their crops. It also might be the theme of Rise in Civilizations because it talks about the village settling in this particular spot.

2. The theme is Political Institutions and Ideas because democracy is a type of government. This could also be the theme of the Rise of Civilizations because it is concerned with how people organize themselves.

3. The theme is Rise of Civilizations because it describes how a civilization became powerful and developed a beautiful society through their wealth. It is also Growth and Change in Societies because the society changed over time.

Show What You Know

1. C
2. C
3. C
4. D
5. A
6. C
7. B

LESSON 2
Studying Ancient History

Lesson Objectives

By the end of this lesson, your student will be able to:

- identify reasons why it is important to study ancient history
- describe methods used by historians to gather and evaluate information
- differentiate between primary and secondary historical resources

Supporting Your Student

Read (Why Study History?)

Help your student understand that people study history for many different reasons. Understanding where things we use today, such as calendars, come from can help us have a greater appreciation for our ancestors. We can also use history as a cautionary tale. By examining what went wrong for civilizations, we can help safeguard our current civilizations from experiencing the same hardships. If we learn to recognize situations that could cause wars or damage the environment, then we can try to prevent them.

Read (Primary and Secondary Sources)

A big misconception about secondary sources is that they are not reliable because the person did not witness the event. Help your student understand that secondary sources can be reliable, but it's important to check that the secondary source is credible. To do this, historians might compare the secondary source to multiple primary or secondary sources of the same event to see if the secondary source is similar.

Practice

Your student may struggle with identifying primary sources beyond those that are written. Remind your student that primary sources can also be artifacts or things that tell about a particular event or civilization. For example, a tool could tell a historian how advanced the civilization's technology was and what resources they had available. They could tell this by looking at the design and materials used to make the tool.

Learning Styles

Auditory learners may enjoy listening to pre-recorded interviews about historical events as primary or secondary sources online or from archived sources at the library.

Visual learners may enjoy looking at artifacts and images about historical events when discussing types of primary sources.

Kinesthetic learners may want to try geocaching to engage in the process of doing research in a physical way.

Extension Activities

Family History

Have your student conduct research into their family history. Have them research primary and secondary sources to find information about their ancestors. They could look at old photos, interview family members, or look at old letters and diaries. Then, have them create a family tree or another visual representation of their research findings.

Primary/Secondary Source Scavenger Hunt

Give your student about 20 to 30 minutes. Have them look around the house to find as many primary and secondary sources as they can about any type of history. It could be the history of an ancient civilization or their own family history. When the time is up, have your student sort the sources into primary and secondary sources.

Answer Key

Write *(Why do you think historians like to use primary sources in their research? What can secondary sources tell historians about an event?)*

- Historians like to use primary sources because they are created at the time of the event, and they are created by a person involved in the event.
- Secondary sources give historians another person's interpretation of what happened at an event, allowing them to see the event from someone else's perspective.

Practice

Answers will vary. Possible answers:

Primary sources: diaries, speeches, letters, maps, photographs, tools, clothing, art, literature, architecture

Secondary sources: books, encyclopedia, articles

Show What You Know

1. B
2. A
3. B
4. A
5. Historians
6. A, B, D
7. Answers will vary. Possible answers: Historians study history to learn more about the world around them and to understand where certain things we have come from. People also study history so they can try to prevent negative events of the past from happening in the future by making necessary changes or different decisions. In addition, people can learn from positive events of the past so that similar actions can be repeated.

LESSON 3
The Importance of Archaeology

Lesson Objectives

By the end of this lesson, your student will be able to:

- describe the process used by archaeologists to draw conclusions about ancient civilizations
- identify types of information that can be learned from archaeology
- recognize examples of early written records

Supporting Your Student

In the Real World
One way you can assist your student with this activity would be to use sand, potting soil, and other types of soil for digging. Layer these in a large container. Hide small objects in the soil and sand for your student to find.

Read *(Excavating a Site)*
As your student reads the steps that archaeologists use to excavate a site, encourage them to create a list of steps. This will help them when they complete the Practice activity and can be beneficial for helping them understand how thorough archaeologists must be to preserve artifacts.

Read *(Written Records)*
To help your student visualize and connect with the written records in this section, compare hieroglyphics to today's use of emojis. Each emoji represents a word, idea, or feeling. When people use emojis in emails or text messages, it serves as a symbol for something just like the hieroglyphics.

Learning Styles

Auditory learners may enjoy listening to an archaeologist describe their day through an online podcast or video.

Visual learners may enjoy looking at the different pictures of the artifacts that are found online.

Kinesthetic learners may enjoy dividing up an area of land into a grid using string and wooden pegs or stakes as if they were an archaeologist.

Extension Activities

Writing Your Own Hieroglyphics
Have your student design their own form of hieroglyphics using pictures or symbols to represent words and ideas. Your student may create a message in their hieroglyphics, and you can figure out the message.

Backward Artifacts
Have your student look at the facts below about specific ancient civilizations or research other facts about ancient civilizations. Then have your student describe what artifact could be found that would support each fact discovered about that civilization.

- The Aztecs had floating gardens.
- Currency was used in ancient China.
- Makeup was worn by many women in ancient Egypt.
- Toothpaste was used in ancient Egypt.

Answer Key

Write *(Choose two of the earliest written records: oracle bones, hieroglyphics, and cuneiform. Write one way they are the same and one way they are different.)*

Answers may vary. Possible answers:

All three—the oracle bones, hieroglyphics, and cuneiform—were ways of communicating with the people in the civilization and allowed historians to learn about their culture. They were written in pictures or symbols that represented words, letters, or ideas.

One of the main differences is that they all came from different civilizations because the oracle bones came from ancient China, hieroglyphics came from ancient Egypt, and cuneiform came from ancient Mesopotamia. Also, they were written on different items and by different methods. Oracle bones were written on bones, hieroglyphics were often written on papyrus, and cuneiform was often carved into tablets.

Practice

6: Clean and catalog each individual artifact.

8: Describe the results from the observations.

1: Analyze historical maps of known whereabouts of the Lumbee tribe in North Carolina.

2: Locate the specific Lumbee area of the excavation site to dig using the Geographic Information System.

5: Place each Lumbee artifact in a bag.

7: Study the Lumbee artifact and document any observations made.

3: Divide the dig site into a grid of boxes for a map to be drawn.

4: Analyze each layer of soil for artifacts left behind from the Lumbee tribe.

Show What You Know

1. 4: Place artifacts in bags and catalog them.
   1: Research where the dig site is using maps, records, surveys, and the GIS.
   5: Make observations about the artifacts and determine what they can reveal about the civilization.
   3: Look between each layer of soil for artifacts.
   2: Excavate the site.

2. Answers will vary. Possible answers: clothing, tools, weapons, food, goods for trading, belief systems, politics, recreation, laws, behaviors

3. B: oracle bones
   C: cuneiform
   A: hieroglyphics

Lesson Objectives

By the end of this lesson, your student will review the following big ideas from Chapter 1.

- Archaeologists uncover artifacts that tell them about ancient civilizations and cultures. (Lesson 1)
- Common themes in history help us understand and interpret history. (Lesson 1)
- Historians gather and evaluate information from primary and secondary sources. (Lesson 2)
- Archaeologists have a specific process they use to analyze and draw conclusions about ancient civilizations. (Lesson 3)

Supporting Your Student

Write *(If historians and archaeologists were to study us in the future, what themes would they notice?)*

Support your student by asking the following guiding questions:

- How does the internet and social media fit into one of these common themes?
- How do we interact with our environment? Land? Water? Weather?
- What kind of government does our society have? What artifacts might demonstrate this?
- What traditions or customs does your community have? What would archaeologists possibly find some day as evidence?
- How is our society growing and changing?
- What is the geography of your community?

Review *(Primary and Secondary Sources)*

After reviewing the images of the Declaration of Independence and encyclopedias, challenge your student to come up with other examples of primary and secondary sources. Ask your student to tell you why historians would use both sources when analyzing the past.

Practice *(History Themes Mind Map)*

Support your student with the following guiding questions:

- What does the fact that this is a French coin found in Russia tell us about the interconnectedness of societies at that time or the growth of societies? You could mention that this shows these areas may have traded with each other or people moved between the countries.
- Does the image of the crown tell us anything about governments? You could mention that it shows a ruler on it.
- Does the fact the coin was found next to a port on the sea tell us anything? You could mention that this meant people used ships to travel between the two countries.
- What do you think this coin was traded for?
- How could this coin have ended up in Russia? You could mention that some people from the region of France traveled to or traded with someone from the Russian area.
- What is the significance of a port on the large body of water? You could mention that this means that the area engaged in a lot of trading to have an established area to receive ships.

Practice *(Plan a Five-Paragraph Essay)*

Support your student in coming up with main ideas by asking the following guiding questions:

- How do historians use common themes while researching the past?
- How do archaeologists help historians?
- Why are artifacts important?
- How do historians use primary and secondary sources?
- What do historians do with all the information they gather?

Learning Styles

Auditory learners may enjoy watching and listening to a video about archeology and how historians use artifacts to study the past.

Visual learners may enjoy looking at pictures of ancient artifacts at a museum or online.

Kinesthetic learners may enjoy acting as an archaeologist and pretending to work at an excavation site. They could choose an area in your yard to try and dig up artifacts. It may be helpful to bury some items beforehand for your student to discover.

Extension Activities

Create a Multimedia Presentation
Ask your student to create a multimedia presentation summarizing this chapter. Make sure they have slides dedicated to the common themes of history, the importance of archeology and artifacts, primary and secondary sources, and the process archaeologists and historians use to analyze the past. Encourage your student to use the internet to find images to include in their presentation.

Scavenger Hunt
Visit a local museum (in person or virtually) and look at artifacts on display. Discuss with your student what common history themes these artifacts tell us about a society. Find at least five artifacts in your museum and write entries in a journal describing each object. Remind your student this is similar to how archaeologists catalog artifacts they find.

Answer Key

Write *(If historians and archaeologists were to study us in the future, what themes would they notice?)*
Answers will vary. Possible answers: The internet and social media show how our society is interconnected. How we sell and buy items all across the world shows the interconnectedness of our society. In the United States, there is a democratic government which fits into the theme of development of political institutions and ideas. Our society celebrates holidays which is the theme of belief systems. Your student may describe the geography of where they live. Your student may describe their own traditions and customs.

Practice *(Vocabulary - Three's a Crowd)*
1. Catalog: Since cuneiform and hieroglyphics were both writing systems for ancient civilizations, catalog does not belong because it is what archaeologists do with artifacts after they have been excavated.

2. Scribe: Since historian and archaeologists are both people who study the past, a scribe does not belong because it is someone who keeps records or writes text.

3. Ancestors: Since GIS and excavate are both parts of what archaeologists use and do when looking for artifacts, ancestors does not belong because they are people in your family who lived long ago.

4. Secondary source: Since artifacts are an example of a primary source, secondary source does not belong because it is not directly related to the original event.

5. History: Since artifacts and oracle bones are objects studied in history, history does not belong because it is the study of the past.

Practice *(History Themes Mind Map)*
Answers will vary. Possible answers:

- Interconnectedness of Societies: money being traded across civilizations, people traveling to different civilizations
- Development of Political Institutions and Ideas: crown on coin shows what type of government the French had
- Growth and Change in Societies: civilizations expanded, French moved into Russia at some point, if there was money then there were probably different economic classes
- Rise of Civilization: money and travel show people organizing into different societies
- Human Environment Interactions: used the Caspian Sea as a way to travel between countries, society built a port at the sea to use for trading
- Geography: coin found next to a sea, found east of where the coin came from, France and Russia as places

Practice *(Plan a Five-Paragraph Essay)*
Answers will vary. Make sure your student covers the common themes of history, primary and secondary sources, and the process used by archaeologists and historians.

Quick Review

Refer to the statement your student circled in the Show What You Know section to self-assess their knowledge of the chapter concepts. Then to assist in determining if your student is ready to take the assessment, consider:

- Having your student list all seven common themes of history. Ask your student to describe each theme and discuss possible examples of each theme. For geography, ask your student to list and describe the five themes of geography.
- Having your student discuss the difference between a primary and secondary source. Discuss with your student examples of both sources.
- Having your student describe the importance of artifacts and the process archaeologists and historians use to analyze the past.

14

Discover! SOCIAL STUDIES • GRADE 6 • CHAPTER 1 ASSESSMENT

Chapter Assessment

Fill in the blanks using the vocabulary words in the Word Bank below.

Word Bank   excavate   catalog   cuneiform   GIS   archaeology   artifacts   ancestors

1._____ is the study of the things of the past that people made, used, and left behind to understand how they lived.

2. The archaeologist will _____, or make a list, of the bones and tools they found at the site of an ancient civilization.

3. Archaeologists _____ an ancient ruins site in Mexico by gently digging in the ground.

4. Before archaeologists start digging, they can use the _____ database of maps to find the best location.

5. _____ are the things of the past that people made, used, and left behind.

6. In ancient Mesopotamia, historians study clay tablets with _____ writings.

7. Historians look for common themes in how our _____ built and organized civilizations.

8. Describe the difference between primary and secondary sources.

....
....
....
....

9. List the common themes of world history.

....
....
....
....

10. Why is it important to study ancient history? Circle all correct answers.

   A. To learn from mistakes societies made in the past

   B. To understand the world around us

   C. To pass middle school

   D. To understand movies we watch about the past

   E. To learn from our ancestors

11. List the steps in the process archaeologists use to gather and study artifacts.

....

....

....

....

12. Which step does not belong in how historians collect information?

    A. Study primary and secondary sources

    B. Take notes

    C. Ask questions

    D. Summarize findings

    E. Make opinions on whether a society is smart or not

    F. Write reports on conclusions

Chapter Assessment Answer Key

1. Archeology

2. catalog

3. excavate

4. GIS

5. Artifacts

6. cuneiform

7. ancestors

8. Answers may vary. Possible answers: Primary sources are original sources from a period in history. Primary sources are written first-hand by a witness to an event. Secondary sources are an interpretation, summary, or an analysis of one or more primary sources. They are written by someone without witnessing the event.

9. Answers may vary. Possible answers: Geography, Human-Environment Interactions, Rise of Civilization, Growth and Change in Societies, Development of Political Institutions and Ideas, Belief Systems, and Interconnectedness of Societies

10. A, B, E

11. Answers may vary. Possible answers: They find the site of an ancient civilization using the Geographic Information Systems (GIS). They excavate the site. As they dig through different layers of the soil, they clean and bag any artifacts found. They send artifacts off to a lab to be analyzed and cataloged.

12. E

Alternative Assessment

Project: Make a Documentary

Project Requirements or Steps:

2. Find two items in your house that could be artifacts for future archaeologists to find. These objects could be a dish, a coin, a phone, a book, a pen, a watch, etc.

3. Think about the following:

   A. How each item tells a story that fits into a common theme in history

   B. The steps in the archeology process

   C. How an archaeologist would find and analyze these artifacts

   D. How a historian would draw conclusions from these artifacts.

4. Write a script.

5. Use props around your house to set the scenes needed for your documentary.

6. Ask a parent or other family member to help you film your documentary.

7. Present your documentary and explain the differences between primary and secondary sources.

Alternative Assessment Rubric

Use the following rubric to grade your student's assessment.

	4	3	2	1	Points
Content	The content is relevant to the chapter and very informative.	The content is relevant to the chapter and informative.	The content is only slightly relevant to the chapter and somewhat informative.	The content is not relevant or informative.	
Creativity	The documentary is creatively written and exceeds expectations.	The documentary is creatively written.	The documentary shows a little creativity.	The documentary is not creative.	
Delivery	The documentary is delivered clearly and was well rehearsed.	The documentary is delivered clearly with one or two mistakes.	The documentary is delivered with several mistakes.	The documentary has a distracting number of mistakes that prevent the audience from understanding the overall message.	
Grammar and Mechanics	The documentary does not contain any grammar errors.	The documentary contains one or two grammar errors.	The documentary contains a few grammar errors.	The documentary has a distracting number of grammar errors.	

Total Points _____/16

Average _____

Lesson Objectives

By the end of this lesson, your student will be able to:

- describe the characteristics of a civilization
- explain how Sumer advanced from farming villages into cities
- explain how the Tigris and Euphrates Rivers created fertile soil
- describe techniques used to effectively control and use rivers

Supporting Your Student

Explore

If your student struggles with identifying differences between the two photos of the modern city and ancient city, they may benefit from thinking aloud about details they notice in each picture and then identifying differences between the details they came up with. If your student struggles to get started, point out one detail from one picture that you notice (such as the architecture) and prompt them to point out a detail related to yours in the other picture. Take a moment to discuss the differences between these details before moving on to other details that your student notices. For example, your student might notice that the buildings in the modern city are taller and made of different materials than the buildings in the ancient city.

Write *(How did Sumer grow from a group of farming villages into a civilization of city-states?)*

Encourage your student to review the characteristics of a civilization and identify one of the characteristics found in Sumer. Ask them to think about how Sumer grew to have this characteristic. This should help your student make the connection between the two. For example, there is a government with leaders in a civilization. The priest-kings were the leaders of city-states. Additionally, point out that people in civilizations usually have different jobs that support parts of the civilization, such as farming, building structures, trading, etc. As people were organized to work different jobs besides farming, city-states grew and developed because there were opportunities for people to focus on something other than having to farm for their necessary food. People could depend on each other to provide different things the community or civilization needed.

Practice

Your student may struggle to understand the purpose of the irrigation system in the photo. Remind them that an irrigation system is used to move water from one location to another. Guide them to see that farmers might have needed irrigation systems in Sumer to grow crops because the area was very dry. Discuss what jobs could have contributed to the building of the irrigation system by examining the structure and asking leading questions, such as "What does it look like the irrigation system is made of?," "How do you think the materials got there?," "Did someone need to cut or shape the rock?," and "Did someone need to make the tools that the people used to build the irrigation system?" Help your student connect the irrigation system to characteristics of a civilization by pointing out that this might be a structure seen in urban centers, as well as how it required people working different jobs to create it.

Learning Styles

Auditory learners may enjoy listening to audio clips of water running through a dam or canal or the sounds of a bustling city. Then they can imagine how those sounds might have been the same or different in an ancient civilization.

Visual learners may enjoy viewing how irrigation systems work. You can go online and find videos of dams and canals in action or research maps of river systems to see how water can be manipulated to help people.

Kinesthetic learners may enjoy sketching or planning out an irrigation system for a major body of water nearby. You may want to have your student imagine how irrigation might be used to control water from a river, lake, or ocean they know.

Extension Activities

Create a Civilization

Consider having your student create their own civilization. Encourage them to identify architecture, select a language, and determine jobs for the various citizens of their civilization. Your student could sketch designs of the civilization or mold the city plans out of clay.

Make an Irrigation Model

Consider having your student create their own irrigation model. Use a tub and identify one area of the tub as a "water source" where water will be added. Direct your student to use clay, cardboard, or other materials to divert a flow of water in different directions. Have your student start with one path of water and then have them create branches of irrigation off of the main source of water. Allow your student to pour water into their model to see how they have controlled the water flow.

Answer Key

Explore

Answers may vary. Possible answers: I see the tall buildings. There are probably a lot of people and noise. The ancient city looks different from the modern city because the buildings are shorter and look like they are made of something different.

Write *(How did Sumer grow from a group of farming villages into a civilization of city states?)*

Answers may vary. Possible answer: Sumer grew from a group of farming villages into a civilization of city-states by organizing the people to work different jobs other than farming.

Write *(How did people in ancient civilizations control and use rivers to help them? How do we control and use water in our current civilizations to help us?)*

Answers may vary. Possible answer: Ancient civilizations controlled water by creating irrigation systems, including dams and canals, to move the water where they wanted it to go. We control water now with plumbing, like sinks and sprinkler systems.

Practice

Answers may vary. Possible answers:

1. An irrigation system like the one in the picture would help farmers get water into different areas of the field.
2. Using water from a river would help people in a civilization grow more crops and have easier access to water if they live in a dry area.
3. People might need to create the canals to help move the water out toward the edges of the picture.
4. This irrigation system could be a type of unique structure or architecture seen in an urban center. It also required people with different jobs to create it, such as people to carve the land and rock and people to make the tools to do the work.

Show What You Know

1. A, B, D, E
2. False
3. B
4. Answers may vary. Possible answer: Sumer controlled the Tigris and Euphrates Rivers to help them by creating an irrigation system of dams and canals to get the river water to more parts of the land.
5. Answers may vary. Possible answer: The silt that was moved from the Tigris and Euphrates Rivers by the irrigation systems helped create fertile soil.

Lesson Objectives

By the end of this lesson, your student will be able to:

- locate on a map the site of ancient Mesopotamia, modern Iraq, Syria, and surrounding countries
- describe and explain why trade was important in Sumer
- categorize social classes of the Sumerian civilization
- evaluate the role religion had in Sumerians' lives
- describe daily life in Sumer

Supporting Your Student

Explore

This activity is focused on what is important in a student's daily life. The goal is to get your student thinking about what people do in their daily life and why it is important to them. It may help your student get started if you summarize one activity you do each day and why it is important to you. For example, you might say, "I work out every day. This is important to keep my body healthy, so I make sure to do it daily."

Practice

For this activity, your student will need to identify and analyze the religion, trade practices, and social classes of Sumer. If your student struggles to get started with this activity, encourage them first to identify the religion, trade practices, and social classes. Encourage them to go back in the text and highlight information that tells about these aspects of Sumerian life. Additionally, point out how the specifics of what the Sumerians did can show that something was important to them. For example, you could point out how the Sumerians showed that religion was important to them because they built large ziggurats, offered daily sacrifices of meals to their gods, and washed the statues of their gods. If religion wasn't important to them, then they probably wouldn't have done these things.

Online Connection

This activity asks your student to select a modern-day city that exists in the area where Sumer used to be. It may help to search for a current political map of Iraq and direct your student to find Baghdad and the Persian Gulf so they have an idea of which cities fall within the area where Sumer was located.

Learning Styles

Auditory learners may enjoy listening to the pronunciation of terms like "ziggurat" and "Baghdad." Consider searching the audio pronunciation of these terms to support understanding during the reading portion of the lesson.

Visual learners may enjoy seeing more examples of items that were traded by the Sumerians. Consider having students research pictures of the various goods mentioned in the reading portion of the lesson and create a collage of these images. They could also compare these images to similar items that we have today by noting the visual similarities and differences.

Kinesthetic learners may enjoy molding a ziggurat out of clay to imagine how the construction process of these important monuments worked.

Extension Activities

Trade Talk

Allow your student to imagine they are going to trade something with you for something you have. Encourage them to pick an item they have that they would like to trade for something you have. Remind your student that they would need to be convincing and the trade would need to make sense. Then, allow them to pretend to trade with you!

Religion Research

In this lesson, your student learned about the Sumerian polytheistic religion. Consider having your student research the various gods of the Sumerian religion to see what kind of ideas the Sumerians found important.

Answer Key

Write *(Where was Mesopotamia and Sumer located? Describe where you could find these two areas.)*

Answers may vary. Possible answers: Mesopotamia was located in modern-day Iraq between the Tigris and Euphrates Rivers. Sumer was located in Mesopotamia, between Baghdad and the Persian Gulf.

Write *(What was life like in Sumer? What did people do every day?)*

Answers may vary. Possible answers: Sumerian people worked their jobs and worshipped their gods. Students from wealthy families went to school. Some people in the upper classes ran their own businesses.

Practice

Answers may vary. Possible answers:

Religion: The Sumerians tried to live their lives to please the gods. The priest-kings tried to guide the people. Sumerians built ziggurats to their gods, offered daily sacrifices, and washed the statues of their gods.

Trade: They would trade cloth, oil, grain, and wine for things they needed like wood and lapis lazuli. Trade was important because it helped the Sumerians gather resources they needed.

Social Class: The social classes were determined by which job people worked.

Show What You Know

1. C

2. B, C

3. Your student should label the map as seen below. Also, your student should color Iraq blue.

4. B: Priest-kings
   A: Upper class
   D: Lower class
   C: Slaves

5. Answers may vary. Possible answers: Trade was important in Sumer because it helped the Sumerians gather new resources they needed.

6. Answers may vary. Possible answers: Sumerian people worked their jobs and worshipped their gods. Students from wealthy families went to school. Some people in the upper classes ran their own businesses.

7. Answers may vary. Possible answers: Religion was important to Sumerians because they believed that the gods affected every part of their lives. They showed that religion was important by building ziggurats, making daily sacrifices to their gods, and washing statues of their gods to keep them happy.

LESSON 7
Ancient Writing

Lesson Objectives

By the end of this lesson, your student will be able to:

- explain how written language developed in Mesopotamia
- describe how records were kept in Sumer
- experience the process of writing cuneiform

Supporting Your Student

Explore

The goal of this activity is to get your student considering how pictures and words share information. Your student may struggle to write about what the picture is showing. If they struggle to get started, ask them to point out details about the picture and guide them toward putting all of these details into sentences.

Write *(How did writing in Mesopotamia change over time?)*

Encourage your student to start by explaining how written language started in Mesopotamia (pictograms) and became a different end result (cuneiform). Direct your student to think about how the two types of language were different and how one changed into the other.

Practice

The goal of this activity is to give your student experience with writing in cuneiform. Your student may feel overwhelmed by writing a whole word in cuneiform and may not know where to start. Consider coming up with a word together, and then encourage your student to work letter by letter.

Learning Styles

Auditory learners may enjoy hearing the correct pronunciation of terms in the reading section, such as "cuneiform" or "stylus." Consider searching for the audio pronunciation of these terms to support understanding during the reading portion of the lesson.

Visual learners may enjoy looking at more pictures of pictograms. Consider searching for images of Egyptian hieroglyphics and pictograms to help your student see the different ways images were used to record ideas.

Kinesthetic learners may enjoy representing language in different ways. Consider having your student represent language about similar topics the Sumerians did—the stars, laws, daily events, or stories. Your student could draw images to represent their ideas, create clay sculptures, or try writing with more cuneiform!

Extension Activities

Create a Cuneiform Clay Tablet

Gather some clay and a writing utensil (you can use a pen, pencil, or crayon). Flatten out the clay and have your student carve some cuneiform letters into the tablet. Have your student use the cuneiform alphabet list below to carve a word into their clay tablet.

Sumerian Cuneiform Alphabet

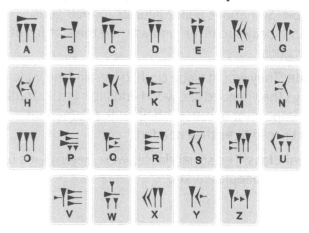

Find the Best Stylus

In this lesson, your student learned about how Sumerians used clay tablets and a stylus to record writing. Today, we use many different items to write: pencils, pens, markers, and crayons! Allow your student to gather a few of these items and practice writing cuneiform with them on paper. Ask your student to rank which writing object is the "best" and which is the "worst." Have a short discussion with your student about which objects they chose and how they seem to be similar to or different from the Sumerian stylus.

Answer Key

Write *(How did writing in Mesopotamia change over time?)*
Answers will vary. Possible answer: Writing in Mesopotamia changed from pictograms to cuneiform letters.

Write *(How did the Sumerians keep records? What are some of the things they chose to keep records of?)*
Answers will vary. Possible answer: The Sumerians kept records on trade, laws, the stars, and daily events, as well as wrote stories. They recorded this information on clay tablets with a stylus.

Practice
Answers will vary. You should use the cuneiform alphabet image to determine if your student correctly depicted their chosen word in cuneiform writing.

Show What You Know
1. True
2. False
3. A, B, C, E, G
4. Writing was recorded in Sumer using clay tablets and a stylus.
5. B

Mesopotamian Inventions

Lesson Objectives

By the end of this lesson, your student will be able to:

- identify Mesopotamian contributions to math and science
- give examples of art thought to be developed by the Mesopotamians
- compare ancient Mesopotamia to modern-day Iraq

Supporting Your Student

Explore

Your student may struggle with identifying ways that people keep time in modern life and why it is important. To help them get started, first discuss ways they keep track of time in their life at home. Once the student has identified some ways they keep track of time, ask them some guiding questions, such as "Why does time matter?" or "Why do you have clocks in your house or car today?"

Write *(What are some similarities between life for the Mesopotamians and modern life in Iraq?)*

Your student may struggle to identify clear connections between ancient Mesopotamia and modern-day Iraq. Encourage your student to start by only thinking about one time period and listing as many details as they can about life during that time period. Then direct your student to repeat this process about the other time period. Once your student has listed details about life in ancient Mesopotamia and modern-day Iraq, guide your student to look for similarities between the two.

Practice

Your student may struggle to identify how an invention is used during modern times. Guide your student to see how these initial inventions have been improved upon or can be part of larger objects today. For example, the wheel the Mesopotamians used was very simple. However, wheels today are a part of many complex machines, like cars, airplanes, the gears in mechanical equipment, and simple mechanisms like the pulleys used to raise and lower blinds on a window.

Learning Styles

Auditory learners may enjoy explaining the purpose of each invention as they learn about them. Consider pausing during the reading sections to allow your student to verbally brainstorm why the inventions were created and what impacts they had on society.

Visual learners may enjoy watching a video of a pottery wheel or other Mesopotamian inventions in action. Consider searching the internet for videos of the various inventions in action.

Kinesthetic learners may enjoy using a pottery wheel to create their own pot.

Extension Activities

Modern-Day Art

Assist your student in learning more about the different types of art the Mesopotamians created. Have your student think about these art forms by asking, "How are they similar? How are they different?" Prompt your student to find one example of a modern form of Mesopotamian art, like a handmade pot, sculpture, or carving, and compare it to what they learned about in today's lesson.

Track the Changes

Have your student select one of the Mesopotamian inventions to learn more about. Prompt your student by asking, "How has this invention and its uses changed over time?" Have your student research how the Mesopotamian version of the invention changed and then create a timeline to show these changes.

Answer Key

Explore

Answers will vary. Possible answer: I use a watch, an alarm clock, or a clock on a phone or computer to keep track of time. The Mesopotamians probably wanted to keep track of time to help them know when to plant and harvest crops or to keep accurate records of events in their history.

Write *(What do you think life would be like without these Mesopotamian inventions? Why do you think these inventions are important?)*

Answers will vary. Possible answer: The Mesopotamians invented the wheel and wheels are used today on cars and buses. Without the wheel, we would not have these modes of transportation that allow us to move quickly from place to place and transport people and goods.

Write *(What are some similarities between life for the Mesopotamians and modern life in Iraq?)*

Answers may vary. Possible answers: Mesopotamia and modern-day Iraq are similar because they both use irrigation to grow crops and get products from other countries through trade.

Practice

Answers will vary. Possible answers:

Wheels: Wheels are used today on cars, buses, airplanes, trains, shopping carts, suitcases, and other objects that need to be moved easily.

Pottery: Pottery is still used today as vases, cups, and bowls. People still make it using pottery wheels.

Maps: Many maps are electronic now, but you can still find paper maps. They help people get from place to place in the world.

Sculptures: Sculptures are placed in museums and in places where people can admire them.

Show What You Know

1. B, D
2. A, C
3. C
4. B, C, D
5. B

Lesson Objectives

By the end of this lesson, your student will be able to:

- analyze the rise and fall in power of the Sumerian civilization
- trace the rise of the Amorite civilization and its development into the Babylonian Empire
- analyze the importance of Hammurabi and Hammurabi's Code

Supporting Your Student

In the Real World

Your student may struggle to identify a leader or what makes someone a "good leader." To assist your student, consider sharing an example of someone you think is a good leader and summarize why you think they are a good leader. Then ask your student to think about someone similar.

Write (How did the Sumerians lose power?)

To answer this question, encourage your student to work backward, starting from when the Sumerians lost their land to the Amorites and moving to when they were powerful. Ask your student guiding questions, such as "What happened before that?" or "What caused that?" This process should guide your student back through what caused the Sumerians to lose their power.

Practice

Your student may struggle to identify direct effects from each event in the chart. Encourage your student to summarize one event at a time. When your student summarizes the event, direct them to think about what happened after the event in order to complete the chart. This direction should help your student identify effects from the initial event. For example, the first event is the expansion of Sumer and its walls. The effect of this event is that another civilization was able to invade because the walls could not be watched and the civilization rapidly expanded.

Learning Styles

Auditory learners may enjoy hearing the correct pronunciations of terms such as "Babylon" or "Hammurabi." Consider searching audio pronunciations of these terms on the internet.

Visual learners may enjoy viewing maps of Mesopotamia and how they changed as different civilizations and empires emerged. Consider searching for maps of Sumer and Babylon to allow your student to see how the events they read about can be visually represented on a map.

Kinesthetic learners may enjoy creating two models of the Sumerian wall—one before the civilization expanded and one after the civilization expanded—to help them identify why the larger civilization was more difficult to protect.

Extension Activities

Create a Timeline

Help your student create a timeline representing the following events in the correct order:

- King Hammurabi made Babylon successful.
- The Amorites created Babylon.
- The Sumerian civilization expanded.
- Babylon lost power.
- The Sumerian civilization was invaded.

A Plan for Power

Have your student imagine they are an ancient ruler who has just conquered a new region. This new land is focused on growing crops and trading. Your student must decide how they will rule this new area. Help them develop a plan by asking, "How will you create an empire?" Their plan should include a drawing of their empire, the crops they will grow, the social structure for their society, their trade plan, and their defense and military plan.

Answer Key

Explore

Answers will vary. Possible answers: Everyone must pick up trash when they see it on the ground. Everyone must volunteer somewhere once a month. Everyone must own a dog.

Write *(How did the Sumerians lose power?)*

Answers may vary. Possible answers: The Sumerians lost power when their civilization became too large to be protected.

Write *(Who was Hammurabi? What did he do to make Babylon more powerful?)*

Answers may vary. Possible answers: Hammurabi was a king of the Babylonian Empire. He created laws and strengthened the military to make Babylon more powerful.

Practice

Cause	Effect
The Sumerian civilization expanded and had to build a larger wall.	The Sumerians could not protect their entire civilization, which allowed another civilization to invade them.
The Sumerians were invaded by a different civilization and were very unstable.	The Sumerians lost control of their land and the empire of Babylon was created.
Hammurabi became king of the empire of Babylon.	Hammurabi created a set of laws called the Code of Hammurabi and strengthened Babylon's military.

Show What You Know

1. D
2. D
3. A
4. A, C
5. A

Lesson Objectives

By the end of this lesson, your student will review the following big ideas from Chapter 2.

- Sumer can be classified as a civilization because the people lived in a more advanced manner with a shared language and a variety of jobs for people to work. (Lesson 5)
- Daily life in Sumer included work, time with family, and religion. (Lesson 6)
- Written language started in Mesopotamia as pictograms and eventually developed into a script with letters called cuneiform. (Lesson 7)
- The Mesopotamians made contributions to math, science, and art, such as a counting system, the wheel, a way to keep time, and pottery. (Lesson 8)
- Sumerian culture rose to power quickly as they expanded their civilization and fell when it had grown so large that other civilizations invaded. (Lesson 9)

Supporting Your Student

Practice (Which Doesn't Belong?)

Encourage your student to state the definitions of each word in a group. Then have them discuss how the definitions might be related by focusing on common words or themes found between two of them. For example, pictograms and cuneiform are both forms of writing or language, while a ziggurat has nothing to do with language. Therefore, ziggurat is the word that does not belong.

Practice (Timeline)

Your student may have trouble putting all of the events in order on the first try. Direct your student to write the different events on note cards or slips of paper and then have your student try putting the events in order. Allow your student to move events around until they feel the timeline is complete with all of the events from the list. Then direct your student to record their ideas on the timeline.

Practice (Cause and Effect)

To help your student complete this activity, encourage your student to summarize one event at a time. When your student summarizes the event, direct them to think about what happened in the world after the event from the chart. This direction should help your student identify effects from the initial event.

Learning Styles

Auditory learners may enjoy discussing their ideas about what made Sumer successful.

Visual learners may enjoy completing online research to find images of the different inventions the Mesopotamians created.

Kinesthetic learners may enjoy pretending to trade goods with you to practice how trade worked in ancient Mesopotamia.

Extension Activities

Jobs in Sumer

Have your student imagine they live in Sumer. What would their job be? What would a day in their life be like? What kind of items would they use? Have them write a diary entry from a day in their Sumerian life.

Ancient vs. Modern Day

Have your student research what daily life is like in modern-day Iraq, including the various cultures that live there. Ask your student to focus on the following questions: How is it similar to daily life in Mesopotamia? How is it different? Then have them give an oral presentation about their findings.

Answer Key

Write *(What are two things you think made Sumer successful? How did these things help the civilization grow?)*

Answers will vary. Possible answer: The Sumerians used the rivers to water their crops, which helped them grow extra food,. They also used the rivers to trade with other civilizations, which helped them get items they could not make themselves.

Practice *(Which Doesn't Belong?)*

1. Ziggurat: Ziggurat does not belong because it does not have anything to do with writing.

2. Polytheism: Polytheism does not belong because it does not have anything to do with geography.

3. Script: Script does not belong because it does not have anything to do with civilizations.

4. Empire: Empire does not belong because it does not have anything to do with art.

5. Lapis lazuli: Lapis lazuli does not belong because it does not have anything to do with Sumerian religion.

Practice *(Timeline)*

The events should be listed in the following order on the timeline:

1. The Sumerians settled between the Tigris and Euphrates Rivers.

2. Sumer expanded by taking control of land from other civilizations.

3. The Amorites took control of Sumerian land.

4. The Amorites created the Babylonian Empire.

5. King Hammurabi created laws.

6. King Hammurabi died.

7. The Babylonian Empire lost power.

Practice *(Cause and Effect)*

Answers may vary. Possible answers:

Cause	Effect
Mesopotamians lived between the Tigris and Euphrates Rivers.	The Mesopotamians were able to use the water for irrigation and grow extra crops.
Sumer's leaders organized the people to work different jobs.	The Sumerians could trade with other countries and create new things.
Sumer expanded over time and gained control of land from other civilizations.	The Sumerians could not watch the wall surrounding their civilization and were invaded.

Quick Review

Refer to the statement your student circled in the Show What You Know section to self-assess their knowledge of the chapter concepts. Then to assist in determining if your student is ready to take the assessment, consider:

• Having your student describe the area where Sumer was located on the map of Mesopotamia below.

• Having your student list the different details that make a civilization.

• Having your student summarize the Sumerians' inventions.

Chapter Assessment

2. How did the Tigris and Euphrates help create fertile soil?

   A. They carried seeds for the crops the Sumerians grew.

   B. They dried up and created rich soil for growing crops.

   C. They carried fertile soil and regularly flooded to spread the soil.

3. How did religion guide life in Sumer?

   A. They only practiced their religion one day a week.

   B. The Sumerians prayed to one god.

   C. All of the Sumerians' actions were focused on pleasing the gods.

4. What supplies were used to record cuneiform?

   A. pen and paper

   B. stylus and clay tablet

   C. paint and rock

5. What is one example of Mesopotamian art?

   A. painting

   B. pottery

   C. graffiti

6. Why was trade important in Sumer? Circle all correct answers.

   A. It allowed them to get items they could not produce themselves.

   B. It allowed them to give away extra food they had for free.

   C. It allowed them to travel to new lands.

7. How are ancient Mesopotamia and modern-day Iraq similar?

   A. both use cuneiform

   B. both use irrigation to grow crops

   C. both only build cities surrounded by walls

Read each sentence. Circle True or False.

8. True or False   Irrigation helped ancient people control rivers and use their water.

9. True or False   Cuneiform was used for many reasons in Sumer, but it was not used to keep records of trade.

10. True or False   During his time as king of the Babylonian Empire, Hammurabi created the first written code of laws and strengthened the Babylonian military.

11. Using the map below, label where ancient Mesopotamia, modern Iraq, and modern Syria are located.

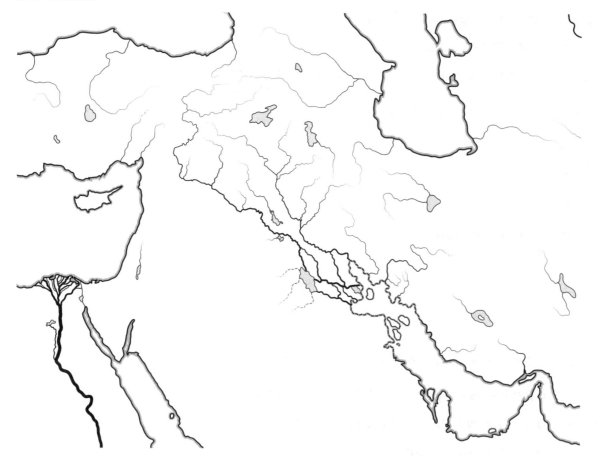

12. Select all of the characteristics of a civilization. Circle all correct answers.

   A. common language

   B. urban center

   C. government leaders

   D. different jobs for people to work

   E. trade

   F. unique architecture

13. Match the Sumerian social class to its role in society.

_____ priests

_____ upper class

_____ lower class

_____ slaves

A. required to work for no pay

B. in charge of making sure the people behaved in a way that would please the gods

C. worked in other people's businesses

D. owned businesses and lived in large homes

14. Circle all of the Mesopotamian inventions.

A. wheel

B. fire

C. counting system

D. silk

15. Put the stages of writing development in order by numbering them 1 (first) to 3 (last).

_____ pictograms

_____ spoken communication with no writing

_____ cuneiform

16. Put the events that led to the Babylonian Empire in order by numbering them 1 (first) to 6 (last).

_____ The Amorites took over Sumer.

_____ Sumer was created.

_____ The Babylonian Empire was created.

_____ Sumer was invaded.

_____ Sumer expanded by taking land from other civilizations.

_____ The Amorites slowly migrated into Sumer.

Chapter Assessment Answer Key

1. C
2. C
3. B
4. B
5. A, C
6. B
7. True
8. False
9. True
10.

11. A, B, C, D, E, F
12. B: priests
    D: upper class
    C: lower class
    A: slaves

13. A, C
14. 2: pictograms
    1: spoken communication with no writing
    3: cuneiform

15. 5: The Amorites took over Sumer.
    1: Sumer was created.
    6: The Babylonian Empire was created.
    3: Sumer was invaded.
    2: Sumer expanded by taking land from other civilizations.
    4: The Amorites slowly migrated into Sumer.

Alternative Assessment

Project: Diary

Project Requirements or Steps:

For this project, you will complete a diary entry where you pretend to be a person living in Sumer. A diary is a daily record of personal thoughts, feelings, and important events. Write about a day in your life using information you know about how people lived in Sumer, including:

- Details about daily life, such as work, family life, and religion
- How you use different inventions, such as the wheel, the base-60 number system, and cuneiform
- Information about what you notice that shows your civilization is successful
- Your fictional name at the bottom of the entry

Alternative Assessment Rubric

Use the following rubric to grade your student's assessment.

	4	3	2	1	Points
Creativity and Neatness	The diary is presented very neatly and the topic shows creativity and originality.	The diary is presented neatly and the topic is somewhat original and creative.	The diary is basic and somewhat neat.	The diary is not neat or creative.	
Quality of Content	The content of the diary is personal and reveals the author's thoughts and feelings. It is very detailed and interesting.	The content of the diary is somewhat personal and talks briefly about the author's thoughts and feelings. It has a few details and is somewhat interesting.	The content of the diary isn't very personal and has only one or two comments about the author's thoughts and feelings. It is not interesting.	The diary is not personal or interesting.	
Connections	The diary makes clear and repetitive connections to the chapter.	The diary is connected to the chapter.	The diary is somewhat connected to the chapter.	The diary is not connected to the chapter.	
Grammar and Mechanics	The diary has no grammar issues and uses advanced vocabulary.	The diary contains a few grammar mistakes and uses age-appropriate vocabulary.	The diary contains several grammar mistakes and uses age-appropriate vocabulary.	The diary contains a distracting number of grammar mistakes and uses overly simplified vocabulary.	

Total Points _____/16

Average _____

38

Discover! SOCIAL STUDIES • GRADE 6 • CHAPTER 2 ASSESSMENT

Geography of Ancient Egypt

Lesson Objectives

By the end of this lesson, your student will be able to:

- find the following locations on a map: Egypt, the Mediterranean Sea, the Nile River, and the Sahara Desert
- describe geographic barriers that fended off invasions into Egypt
- explain how the Egyptians depended on the floodwaters of the Nile for survival
- identify key ways the Nile River influenced Egyptian culture

Supporting Your Student

Read (Geographic Barriers That Protected Egypt)

Your student might not be able to comprehend the true size of the Sahara Desert because it is so much larger than anything they may have experienced. Help them understand this by explaining that the Sahara is larger than the continental United States. It may even help to use online maps for comparison. Additionally, this may be challenging when viewing certain map projections. Explain to your student that map projections can distort the true size of something.

Read (The Nile River and Egyptian Irrigation)

The creation of settlements along rivers was quite common in ancient civilizations, as a water source was crucial for survival. You can deepen your student's understanding by making the connection to Mesopotamia's dependence on the Tigris and Euphrates. In the same way, ancient Egypt depended on the Nile and the fertile soil that was created by these rivers.

Write (How did the Nile impact the culture of ancient Egypt?)

Encourage your student to go back to the sections on the page and highlight examples of how the Nile impacted the daily life of Egyptians. For example, the presence of papyrus allowed them to create a type of paper to write on. Guide your student to see that the ability to write information down and easily carry it with you would have been important when documenting events or keeping business records.

Learning Styles

Auditory learners may enjoy creating a guide to Egyptian physical features that could be recorded and then played back for your student's family.

Visual learners may enjoy creating a virtual flipbook of images depicting Egyptian culture using online images.

Kinesthetic learners may enjoy building a model of Egyptian geographical features such as modeling clay into the shape of the Nile River.

Extension Activities

Create Your Own Map

Have your student create his or her own map of Egypt. Be sure to have them include the following key physical features: the Mediterranean Sea, the Nile River, and the Sahara Desert. Have your student create a map key to deepen their understanding about the size of the Sahara and length of the Nile River. The map could be a simple drawn map or one constructed with paint, construction paper, or other materials.

Create an Acrostic Poem

Have your student create an acrostic poem using the word "Egypt." Each line of the five-line poem should begin with a letter of the country's name. For example, the first line should begin with a word that starts with "E", the second line should begin with a word that starts with "G", and so on. Each line should include a word that describes ancient Egypt and starts with the corresponding letter. For instance, "P" could stand for *papyrus*. The poem should showcase the student's knowledge of the country's physical features, dependence on the floodwaters of the Nile, and the culture of ancient Egypt.

Answer Key

Explore

Answers will vary. Possible answers: I see a desert and pyramids. I wonder who built the pyramids and if anyone lives in the desert.

Write *(Explain how the deserts on both sides of the Nile River protected ancient Egypt.)*

Answers may vary. Possible answers: Few invaders could ever cross the sands to attack Egypt because the deserts proved too great a natural barrier due to their size and the extreme heat.

Write *(How did the Nile impact the culture of ancient Egypt?)*

Answers may vary. Possible answers: Egyptians developed a calendar based on the flooding of the Nile and developed a process that turned papyrus into flattened material that could be written on (also called papyrus).

Practice

1. Israel, Sudan, Libya
2. the Mediterranean Sea, the Red Sea

Show What You Know

1. B
2. C
3. D
4. A, B
5. B: Nile River
   C: Sahara Desert
   A: Mediterranean Sea

Lesson Objectives

By the end of this lesson, your student will be able to:

- identify the two geographic regions that made up ancient Egypt
- describe the Rosetta Stone and why it is important
- explain the importance of papyrus and hieroglyphics to ancient Egyptians

Supporting Your Student

Read (The Two Geographic Regions of Ancient Egypt)

To best support your student through this section, you may want to have them draw the Nile on a piece of paper with arrows pointing north to help them remember that the Nile flows from south to north.

Read (The Importance of Papyrus and Hieroglyphics)

To ensure that your student is focusing on the key information in this text, you could encourage them to underline or highlight key phrases, such as the description of papyrus, the meaning of hieroglyphics, and where hieroglyphics can be found. By doing so, your student will be able to hone in on the most important information on these topics.

Read (The Rosetta Stone)

To help your student understand the incredible impact the Rosetta Stone had in deciphering the written languages of ancient Egypt, you may explain to them that there is now a popular company by the same name that offers courses in mastering foreign languages. By explaining that "Rosetta Stone" is now synonymous with learning new languages, you will help them make the connection regarding the original Rosetta Stone and why the Rosetta Stone changed the way that we are able to study ancient Egypt.

Learning Styles

Auditory learners might enjoy recording a spoken word poem describing the culture of ancient Egypt and then listening to it.

Visual learners might enjoy creating a fake social media post with a picture that explains one of the concepts they learned about today. Based on the picture that they create, the text of the post should help their "followers" better understand the image and deepen their understanding of the culture of ancient Egypt.

Kinesthetic learners may enjoy writing hieroglyphics in clay using a toothpick or craft stick.

Extension Activities

Draw a Cartoon Strip

Have your student draw a cartoon strip with multiple boxes that depicts the discovery of the Rosetta Stone. Include dialogue between the soldiers making the discovery, and reference the importance of the Rosetta Stone in understanding hieroglyphics.

Create a Children's Book

Have your student write a story about papyrus and hieroglyphics to help someone else understand their impact on ancient Egyptian culture. Your student's audience is an elementary-aged child, so be sure they include illustrations and make the book engaging for a young learner.

Answer Key

Explore

Answers may vary. Possible answers: (1st photo) ancient paper, papyrus, ancient scroll, (2nd photo) plants by a river, papyrus plants, crops growing

Read *(The Two Geographic Regions of Ancient Egypt)*

Your student should draw an arrow going from south to north on the map.

Write *(Why is the northern part of Egypt referred to as Lower Egypt?)*

Answers may vary. Possible answers: The northern part is called Lower Egypt because the Nile River flows south to north and the northern portion of Egypt was then downstream.

Write *(Why were papyrus and hieroglyphics important to the culture of ancient Egypt?)*

Answers may vary. Possible answers: The ancient Egyptians used a reed called papyrus that grew near the Nile River to make their paper. With the papyrus, ancient Egyptians were able to record their own written language. It is one of the oldest languages in the world. The ancient Egyptians' written language is called hieroglyphics. The ancient Egyptians did not just use hieroglyphics to write single words. They also used this written language to write long sentences and record their history.

Practice

Answers will vary. Possible answers: pictures of a magnifying glass to show "decoding," or a speech bubble to show language; words and phrases such as "hieroglyphics," "Greek," "decode;" learn about culture

Show What You Know

1. B
2. A
3. B
4. A, C
5. A
6. Top box is labeled Lower Egypt, bottom box is labeled Upper Egypt

Lesson Objectives

By the end of this lesson, your student will be able to:

- explain the significance of religion to the ancient Egyptians
- explain the mummification process
- summarize the history behind and the purpose for a cartouche

Supporting Your Student

Read *(The Significance of Religion to the Ancient Egyptians)*

To help your student better understand the polytheistic religion of the ancient Egyptians, you could have them compare and contrast the beliefs of ancient Egyptians with another religion that they are more familiar with. For example, ask them about the number of gods worshipped in Christianity. How about in Hinduism? How is this similar and different from the religion of ancient Egypt?

Read *(The Mummification Process)*

To best support your student through this section, you could have them number the steps in the mummification process as they read. The process is lengthy and having your student number each step might help them break it down into smaller chunks.

Read *(Cartouche)*

If your student is struggling with this section, remind them that hieroglyphics are symbols that represent words and that hieroglyphics on a cartouche display someone's name. This should help them remember that a cartouche is the name of a pharaoh that is in an oval.

Learning Styles

Auditory learners may enjoy creating rhymes to help them remember key terms from the lesson.

Visual learners may enjoy creating a picture-based guide to explain the process of mummification. They could draw a picture for each step of the mummification process.

Kinesthetic learners may enjoy attempting to mummify a piece of fruit. Search for steps to complete this process online, or pour a mixture of 40 grams of baking soda and 80 grams of salt over apple slices and let them sit in the dark for a week.

Extension Activities

Write a Letter

Have your student pretend that they are a historian who traveled to ancient Egypt to explore the tomb of a pharaoh. Have them write a letter to a friend describing their experience. What did they see? How did it make them feel? How was their experience different from things that they experience in their everyday life?

Draw That Term

Have your student draw pictures representing the vocabulary from the lesson and play a guessing game with them to see if you can correctly identify which terms they have drawn.

Answer Key

Explore

The item is a cartouche and says the name of a person on it. Cartouches were usually buried with pharaohs (the rulers of Egypt). They were important to pharaohs because they thought the cartouche protected them from evil spirits.

Write *(Explain the ancient Egyptians' beliefs about the afterlife.)*

Answers may vary. Possible answers: Ancient Egyptians believed they had the opportunity to become gods when they died, depending on how they lived their life on Earth. The ancient Egyptians believed that when a person died, the person's soul exited the body for a short time. The soul would eventually return to the body after it had been buried, but it needed to be able to find and recognize its body to be able to return to its host.

Write *(Describe the steps involved in the mummification process.)*

Answers may vary. Possible answers: First, the body was embalmed. The ancient Egyptians used oils, chemicals, and tools to remove and preserve organs to prevent the decay of the body. The bodies were washed with water from the Nile River and after 40 days, the organs were wrapped in linen and returned to the body. After the body was embalmed, it was wrapped in linen multiple times to help with preservation. Mummies were eventually placed in a sarcophagus and put in a tomb.

Practice

Answers will vary. Your student may notice that the letter "X" is missing. Because Egyptian hieroglyphics did not match perfectly with the letters in the English language, some letters do not have a hieroglyphic to represent them. Encourage your student to create their own hieroglyphic for the letter "X" if necessary.

Show What You Know

1. A, B, C
2. A
3. B
4. A
5. Answers may vary. Possible answers: First, the body would be embalmed and then it was wrapped. The ancient Egyptians used oils, chemicals, and tools to remove and preserve organs. The bodies were washed with water from the Nile River. Then the organs were wrapped in linen and returned to the body. After the body was embalmed, it was wrapped in linen multiple times. Mummies were eventually placed in a sarcophagus and put in a tomb.

Kingdoms and Rulers of Ancient Egypt

Lesson Objectives

By the end of this lesson, your student will be able to:

- describe the three kingdoms of ancient Egypt
- identify the rulers of ancient Egypt and their contributions to this time
- describe the social pyramid of ancient Egypt

Supporting Your Student

Practice
To best support your student through this section, have them highlight or underline key advancements for each period. Your student could highlight or underline in a different color for each of the time periods so there is a noticeable difference on the page. They could then add the same color coding to the timeline that they make.

Read (Rulers of Ancient Egypt)
You could encourage your student to make flash cards to help them remember the various rulers of ancient Egypt and what each is known for. On the front of each card, your student could write the name of the ruler. Then they could list their accomplishments on the back of the card. They could then move the cards around to put the rulers in chronological order.

Write (Describe the social pyramid of ancient Egyptians.)
To help your student answer the question at the end of this section, have them refer to the pyramid on the page or the graphic on the Explore page. Help your student see that the shape of the pyramid reflects the amount of people in each level of the pyramid. The bottom of the pyramid (slaves, peasants, and servants) made up the bulk of ancient Egypt's population, while only very few people would ever become a priest or government official.

Learning Styles

Auditory learners may enjoy discussing the various rulers and their accomplishments.

Visual learners may enjoy drawing pictures to show what advances were made during each of the time periods of ancient Egypt.

Kinesthetic learners may enjoy creating a three-dimensional model of the social pyramid using craft supplies, such as clay or wooden craft sticks.

Extension Activities

Create a Social Pyramid
Have your student create an ancient Egyptian social pyramid. Have them illustrate the pyramid with a visual representation of each row and label it with a fact about the people who made up that row.

Create a Journal
Have your student write journal entries from the point of view of different members of ancient Egyptian society. Have them explain what life was like for that person based on their place in the social pyramid.

Answer Key

Explore
Answers will vary. Possible answers: I think the people at the top were thought of as more important and probably had a better life than the people at the bottom. I think it was hard to move up the pyramid.

Practice
Timelines should include the Old, Middle, and New Kingdoms. Answers for the facts about the time periods will vary. Possible answers: Egyptians began building the pyramids during the Old Kingdom. During the Middle Kingdom, they traded with the people of Mesopotamia. Horses and chariots became a part of battle during the New Kingdom.

Write *(What were Narmer's contributions to the society of ancient Egypt?)*
Answers may vary. Possible answers: Narmer began to build pyramids, and hieroglyphic writing was developed during his reign.

Write *(Describe the social pyramid of ancient Egyptians.)*
Answers may vary. Possible answer: In ancient Egypt, everyone had a place on the social pyramid. Pharaohs were seen as gods and at the top of the pyramid. Then there were government officials and priests. Underneath them were scribes, followed by artisans, and finally slaves, servants, and peasants.

Show What You Know
1. 2: Middle Kingdom
   3: New Kingdom
   1: Old Kingdom
2. New
3. Middle
4. Slaves, servants, peasants
5. scribes
6. Rameses II
7. Thutmose III
8.

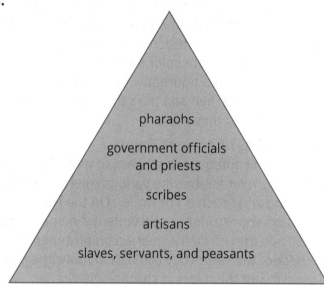

Lesson Objectives

By the end of this lesson, your student will be able to:

- compare and contrast the Kushite and Egyptian civilizations
- identify the two types of written language created by the Kushites
- explain how the kingdom of Kush became wealthy

Supporting Your Student

Read (Kushite and Egyptian Civilizations)

To support your student through this section, have him or her refer back to the previous lessons to better understand the similarities and differences between the ancient civilizations of the Kush kingdom and Egypt. Prompt their thinking with questions about how they each created wealth, how they communicated with each other, and what sort of structures they built.

Read (Written Languages of the Kushites)

To support your student, show them an example of cursive writing so they can better understand how much easier it would be to write in cursive than drawing the detailed symbols of the hieroglyphic-based written language.

Read (How the Kush Became Wealthy)

If your student is struggling with this section, help them better understand the importance of natural resources to the economy in their country. Give them examples of items traded that make their country money. For example, if you live in a mining town, explain how that resource is then processed and sold to other people who need it.

Learning Styles

Auditory learners may enjoy creating a digital recording to describe the similarities and differences of the Kush and Egyptian cultures.

Visual learners may enjoy researching online how to write in Meroitic hieroglyphics and practice writing their name. They can also write their name in Egyptian hieroglyphics and compare the two.

Kinesthetic learners may enjoy creating a replica of the Kush pyramids out of clay.

Extension Activities

Create a Travel Brochure

Your student could create a brochure for someone interested in traveling back in time to visit the ancient kingdom of Kush. The brochure should explain what the traveler can expect to encounter and any points of interest that they might want to see.

Write a Song

Your student could write a song to reinforce the importance of the ancient Kushites, including their languages, religion, and economy. The song can be set to the tune of your student's choice.

Answer Key

Explore
Answers will vary. Possible answers: The carvings look similar because they show carvings of human-like figures. They look very similar, so the civilizations were probably close together and traded ideas and goods.

Write *(Explain how the kingdom of Kush became wealthy.)*
Answers may vary. Possible answer: The kingdom of Kush became very wealthy from trading gold and iron.

Practice
Answers may vary. Possible answers:

(Kushites) located in the northern part of Sudan, had darker skin and shorter hair than the Egyptians, wore animal skins and large earrings, rode directly on their horses, gave more respect to women by allowing them to become rulers

(Egyptians) located in modern-day Egypt and used chariots pulled by horses

(Both) located along the Nile, built temples and pyramids, had written languages and strong governments, traded, were polytheistic

Show What You Know
1. B

2. A, C, D

3. A, C

4. B

5. hieroglyphics, cursive

Lesson Objectives

By the end of this lesson, your student will review the following big ideas from Chapter 3.

- In Africa, the ancient Egyptians relied on the Nile River for many things, including fertile soil for planting crops. They also relied on the Sahara Desert to help keep invaders out. (Lesson 11)
- The Nile River, hieroglyphics, and papyrus were all important to ancient Egyptian culture. (Lesson 12)
- The afterlife was important in Egyptian religion, so many upper class people were mummified. (Lesson 13)
- Ancient Egypt can be divided into the Old Kingdom, the Middle Kingdom, and the New Kingdom, during which different pharaohs ruled over a society based on a social pyramid. (Lesson 14)
- The Kushites and Egyptians were both similar and different. (Lesson 15)

Supporting Your Student

Review *(The Geography and Culture of Ancient Egypt)*

To best support your student throughout this section, have a map of Egypt available for them to look at. There are several maps of Egypt in the lessons within the chapter, or you could provide your own print or online map. Have your student point out the geographic locations of Egypt within Africa, the Nile River, and the Sahara Desert. Having your student find these items on the map can help reinforce these locations, as well as solidify understanding as to why the Nile River and Sahara Desert were important to the ancient Egyptians.

Practice *(Which Doesn't Belong?)*

To help your student with this activity, encourage them to think of a category that they could place two out of the three words in. For example, your student might look at the words *Sahara Desert* and *Nile River* and put them in a category of physical features of Egypt. The other term, *Upper Egypt*, is not a physical feature, so it does not belong.

Practice *(Egyptians vs. Kushites Chart)*

If your student is struggling with what to include in the graphic organizer, have them refer back to Lesson 15. Ask them to use one color to highlight information in the lesson about Egyptians, a second color to highlight information about the Kushites, and a third color to highlight information that applies to both civilizations. Then your student can include this information in the appropriate places on the chart.

Learning Styles

Auditory learners may enjoy discussing the social pyramid of ancient Egypt, including discussing the pros and cons of having a society based on this.

Visual learners may enjoy creating a brochure about ancient Egypt that includes drawings and graphics about its geography, culture, and history.

Kinesthetic learners may enjoy creating a physical timeline by acting out events in Egypt's history, such as developing hieroglyphics or building the pyramids.

Extension Activities

Review Game

Have your student make flash cards with key concepts, terms, and people on one side and a matching description on the other. Play a review game using these cards by showing your student the descriptions while they try to guess the concept, term, and/or person being described, or you can flip them over and show your student the concept, term, and/or person being described and have them give you the description.

Create a Dialogue

Have your student write a conversation between a Kushite and Egyptian. In the dialogue, have them trade information to learn more about the other's culture. How are they similar and how are they different?

Answer Key

Write (Describe the culture and geography of ancient Egypt.)

Answers may vary. Possible answers: Egypt is located in Africa and has important physical features like the Nile River and Sahara Desert. In Egyptian culture, religion was very important. Pharaohs and wealthy people were often mummified and buried in pyramids. Hieroglyphics also allowed Egyptians to keep written records. Overall, Egypt's society was organized by a social pyramid with the pharaoh on top and other classes of people underneath based on their jobs. Most people were part of the bottom level, which included slaves, servants, and peasants.

Practice (Which Doesn't Belong?)

1. Upper Egypt: The other two words are physical features of Egypt, so Upper Egypt does not belong.

2. Polytheism: The other two words are related to writing, so polytheism does not belong.

3. New Kingdom: The other two words are related to the Old Kingdom, so New Kingdom does not belong.

4. Rosetta Stone: The other two words are related to the social pyramid, so Rosetta Stone does not belong.

5. Monotheism: The other two words are related to Kushite religion, so monotheism does not belong.

Practice (Egyptian vs. Kushite Chart)

Answers may vary. Possible answers:

	Egypt	Kush	Similar or Different
Religion	polytheistic	polytheistic	similar
Economy	trading, mining, and farming	trading, mining, and farming	similar
Location	modern-day Egypt on the Nile River	modern-day Sudan on the Nile River	different
Culture	hieroglyphics, developed a calendar, used chariots pulled by horses, and built large pyramids	hair was darker and shorter, Meroitic hieroglyphics and cursive, rode on top of horses, wore animal skins and large pieces of jewelry, and built smaller pyramids	similar and different

Practice (Summarizing the Egyptians vs. Kushites)

Answers will vary. Possible answer: The Kushite civilization was located in the northern part of Sudan, the country just to the south of Egypt. The Kush Kingdom was located along the Nile River, just like the kingdom of ancient Egypt. Much like the ancient Egyptians, the Kushites built temples and pyramids, traded goods with others, farmed, mined, were polythesitc, and developed written languages. Both civilizations also had strong governments. However, there were cultural differences between the two groups. In art from this time period, the Kush are drawn with darker skin and shorter hair than the Egyptians, and the Kush were often wearing animal skins and large earrings. Both groups used horses for transportation, but the Kush rode directly on the horses while the Egyptians used chariots.

Quick Review

Refer to the statement your student circled in the Show What You Know section to self-assess their knowledge of the chapter concepts. Then to assist in determining if your student is ready to take the assessment, consider:

- Having your student look at the map and explain where Egypt is located and how its location impacted the culture of ancient Egypt.
- Having your student identify the advancements that were made during each of the three kingdoms of ancient Egypt and review the natural resources and proximity to water that made the Kushites very wealthy from trade.
- Having your student compare and contrast the ancient civilizations of Kush and Egypt, including their religion, culture, and economy.

Discover! SOCIAL STUDIES • GRADE 6 • CHAPTER 3 ASSESSMENT

51

Chapter Assessment

Match each term to its description.

A. the written languages of the Kushites

2. _____ Sahara Desert

3. _____ Old Kingdom

B. an ancient civilization located along the Nile River in Sudan; its citizens rode horses, wore animal skins, and built smaller pyramids

4. _____ Pharaohs

C. made up the smallest, top portion of the social pyramid

5. _____ Meroitic hieroglyphics and cursive

D. created a natural barrier that helped to protect ancient Egypt from invaders

E. an ancient civilization located along the Nile River; its citizens created a calendar to track the floodwaters of the Nile

6. _____ Egypt

7. _____ Kush

F. a time of great cultural development as Egyptians began building pyramids and developing hieroglyphics

Fill in the blanks with the correct word to complete each sentence.

8. The floodwaters of the _____ River allowed for irrigation of crops in ancient Egypt.

9. The _____ Kingdom was a time of economic growth for ancient Egypt because they began mining and trading with other civilizations.

10. _____ was the first pharaoh of a unified Egypt during the Old Kingdom.

11. The largest portion of the social pyramid was made up of _____.

12. The Egyptians and Kushites practiced a _____ form of religion.

Read each sentence. Circle True or False.

13. True or False   Egypt is located in the northeastern corner of Africa, and the Mediterranean Sea is its border to the north.

14. True or False   During the Middle Kingdom, Egypt grew its empire and won many battles using chariots drawn by horses.

15. True or False   Rameses II was a weak ruler and his reign led to the fall of ancient Egypt.

16. True or False   Natural resources, such as gold and iron, made the ancient Kushites wealthy.

Chapter Assessment Answer Key

1. D
2. F
3. C
4. A
5. E
6. B
7. Nile
8. Middle
9. Narmer
10. peasants/slaves
11. polytheistic
12. True
13. False
14. False
15. True

Discover! SOCIAL STUDIES • GRADE 6 • CHAPTER 3 ASSESSMENT

53

Alternative Assessment

Project: Historical Fiction

Project Requirements or Steps:

Historical fiction is a piece of fictional literature that is based on or around a historical time period or event. For this project, write a short piece of historical fiction based on ancient Egypt.

Be sure to include the following in your story:

- Reference to important aspects of ancient Egyptian culture and geography
- A clear storyline
- A character who is living during the time of the ancient Egyptian civilization

Alternative Assessment Rubric

Use the following rubric to grade your student's assessment.

	4	3	2	1	Points
Accuracy and Relevance	The work has many characteristics or examples that tie it to a historical event or time period. The connections to history are academically advanced and indicate a great deal of effort.	The work has several characteristics or examples that tie it to a historical event or time period.	The work has one or two characteristics or examples that tie it to a historical event or time period.	The work has no connections to history.	
Quality	The work exceeds expectations. The storyline is very interesting and high quality.	The work is of good quality, but there is some room for improvement.	The work has many areas that could be improved.	The work is very low quality.	
Creativity	The work is creative and original and very interesting to the reader.	The work is somewhat creative and original and interesting to the reader.	The work is not very creative or original, but it is interesting to the reader.	The work is not creative or interesting.	
Grammar and Mechanics	The work has no grammar or punctuation issues and uses advanced vocabulary.	The work contains a few grammar or punctuation mistakes and uses age-appropriate vocabulary.	The work contains several grammar and punctuation mistakes and uses age-appropriate vocabulary.	The work contains a distracting number of grammar and punctuation mistakes and uses overly simplified vocabulary.	

Total Points _____/16

Average _____

Discover! SOCIAL STUDIES • GRADE 6 • CHAPTER 3 ASSESSMENT

55

Lesson Objectives

By the end of this lesson, your student will be able to:

- analyze the population growth of the Israelites during their years in Egypt
- describe the Exodus of the Israelites from Egypt
- identify causes and effects of events in Israel's early history

Supporting Your Student

Read *(Jewish Population Growth in Ancient Egypt)*

To best support your student, have them recall the social pyramid of ancient Egypt. The base, by far the largest section of the pyramid, is where the Jewish people would have been. This might help them to better understand the pharaoh's reasoning for controlling the Jewish population in the manner in which he did.

Read *(Exodus of the Israelites From Egypt)*

To help your student conceptualize the Exodus, consider reading sections of the book of Exodus (Chapters 3–13) from the Bible. These chapters outline the plagues in detail, as well as God's promise to protect the Israelites.

Read *(The Ten Commandments)*

Consider reviewing all of the Ten Commandments with your student. Then compare these to the laws written in the Code of Hammurabi. Ask them to identify how the two sets of rules or laws are the same and different. For example, the Code of Hammurabi has a lot more laws than the Ten Commandments. Additionally, the Code of Hammurabi was written for people in Egypt to obey, whereas the Ten Commandments applies to everyone.

Learning Styles

Auditory learners may enjoy creating a recording of themselves telling the story of the early Israelites.

Visual learners may enjoy studying maps to better understand the Jewish people's journey back to Israel.

Kinesthetic learners may enjoy creating a model of the slabs that the Ten Commandments were written on using clay to make the slabs and wooden craft sticks or toothpicks to carve the Ten Commandments into them.

Extension Activities

Create a Timeline

Have your student create a timeline, digitally or on a piece of paper, to show the important events that impacted the Israelites beginning with the famine that led them to Egypt. Encourage your student to include images or illustrations for each event.

Create a Cartoon

Have your student draw a cartoon depicting one of the events of early Israel's history.

Answer Key

Explore
Answers will vary. Possible answers: I may bring food, water, and good shoes. I may face dehydration, heat, and sandstorms. To solve these problems, I should take lots of water, wear a hat, and take a movable shelter (like a tent) with me.

Write *(Explain Moses' role in the Israelites' Exodus from Egypt.)*
Answers will vary. Possible answer: Moses led the Jewish people out of Egypt during the Exodus.

Practice
Answers will vary. Possible answers:

Cause	Effect
There was a famine in Israel.	The Israelites went to Egypt.
The Israelites were chased by the Egyptian army.	According to accounts in Exodus, God parted the Red Sea to allow the Israelites to escape.
The Israelites wandered the desert for 40 years.	According to accounts in Exodus, God provided Israelites with food and water throughout their time in the wilderness.

Show What You Know
1. famine
2. enslaved
3. Moses
4. manna
5. Torah
6. Commandments
7. C
8. A
9. D
10. B

Lesson Objectives

By the end of this lesson, your student will be able to:

- examine the purpose for the Tabernacle
- analyze the construction of the Tabernacle

Supporting Your Student

Read *(The Purpose of the Tabernacle)*

To best support your student through this section, remind them of the history of the early Israelites. Ask them questions, such as, "Why were the Israelites wandering in the desert?" and "What did the Israelites believe God helped them do?" Connect this prior knowledge from the previous lesson to the purpose of the Tabernacle as a place that God could dwell with His people and where they could worship Him. Remind your student that the Israelites believed God had delivered them from slavery in Egypt and had promised to give them a homeland.

Read *(The Construction of the Tabernacle)*

To best support your student through this section, consider having your student read Exodus 25–31 and 35–40. These chapters of Exodus describe the construction of the Tabernacle and provide additional context, as well as specific details about the Tabernacle, how it was built, and the materials that were used.

Practice

To best support your student through this section, help them search online for a diagram of the Tabernacle to have a better understanding of what they are drawing. An example drawing is shown in the Answer Key section of this guide. As they draw, they should label the different parts of the structure.

Learning Styles

Auditory learners may enjoy describing the different parts of the Tabernacle as they point to them on the diagram they drew.

Visual learners may enjoy watching a virtual tour of Jerusalem to see the ruins of ancient Israel that can be found online.

Kinesthetic learners may enjoy creating a model of the Ark of the Covenant out of clay and other building supplies.

Extension Activities

Children's Book

Have your student explain the purpose and creation of the Tabernacle to another child by creating a children's book. Your student should include images or illustrations to help their audience understand what the Tabernacle looked like, was used for, and why it was built.

Journal

Have your student create a journal from the point of view of Moses explaining the building of the Tabernacle and the Israelites' time moving it around the desert. Have your student create multiple entries over the course of the Israelites' 40 years in the desert.

Answer Key

Take a Closer Look
The priests would wash their hands and feet to cleanse or purify themselves before entering an area to worship God.

Explore
Answers will vary.

Write (Explain the purpose of the Tabernacle.)
Answers may vary. Possible answer: The Israelites built the Tabernacle for worship, believing God's presence would dwell with them in this place.

Write (Describe the construction of the Tabernacle.)
Answers may vary. Possible answers:

- Instructions described in the book of Exodus
- Portable tent with a rectangular-shaped wooden structure
- Draped with curtains of blue, purple, and red fabrics
- Courtyard contained an altar and laver
- First room in the tent was called the Holy Place and held a menorah, table for sacrificial bread, and an altar
- Innermost room was called the Holy of Holies and Held the Ark of the Covenant, manna, and the rod of Aaron

Practice
The diagram should look similar to the image below and should include most of these labeled items: Holy of Holies, Ark of the Covenant, manna, rod of Aaron, menorah, altar, table, and basin.

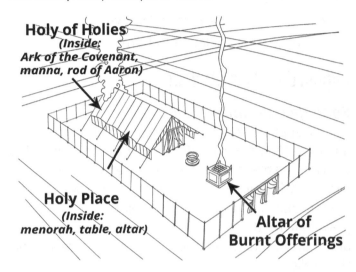

Holy of Holies
(Inside: Ark of the Covenant, manna, rod of Aaron)

Holy Place
(Inside: menorah, table, altar)

Altar of Burnt Offerings

Show What You Know
1. E
2. A
3. F
4. G
5. C
6. D
7. B
8. B

Lesson Objectives

By the end of this lesson, your student will be able to:

- identify the important times of worship held by the Israelites
- recognize the significance of Passover
- describe features of Jewish culture

Supporting Your Student

Read (Jewish Times of Worship)

To best support your student through this section, encourage them to consider ways that people worship who are unable to attend a traditional worship service. Ask your student, "Are there other ways that a person could feel connected to their God?" A healthy prayer life for the Jewish people is a form of worship and is often considered the most important aspect of their religion.

Read (Passover)

To best support your student through this section, have your student underline or highlight the reasoning for Passover and the ways in which it is celebrated. This festival is important to Jewish culture and dates back to the time of the Jewish people living in ancient Egypt. By having your student underline or highlight the reasons that Passover came to be, they will have a much deeper understanding of its importance to Jewish culture.

Read (Jewish Culture)

To best support your student through this section, talk through aspects of your student's culture prior to starting the reading: "What holidays do we celebrate? What traditions do we follow?" Then explain to them that every culture has aspects that are unique to those people. As they read, they should underline or highlight aspects of Jewish culture that are unique to Jewish people, such as their prayer life, rules about eating, celebrations, and holidays.

Learning Styles

Auditory learners may enjoy listening to a recording of a synagogue service online.

Visual learners may enjoy watching videos and looking at pictures of Jewish holidays and festivals online to see how Jewish people celebrate those events.

Kinesthetic learners may enjoy playing games with a dreidel, which can be purchased online, to experience an aspect of Jewish culture.

Extension Activities

Taste Test

Have your student research and prepare unleavened bread. Your student should consider these questions:

- What does it taste like? Would you want to replace leavened bread (like sandwich bread) with unleavened bread regularly?
- Do you think it was hard to be exiled and unable to make and eat your usual bread?
- Why do you think this food holds such significance for Jewish people?

Coming of Age

Have your student dig deeper into the traditions of bat and bar mitzvahs. How does one prepare for this event, how is it celebrated, and what is the history? Then, have your student research other similar celebrations, like sweet 16 parties or quinceañeras, to compare and contrast the ways different cultures and traditions honor a young person coming of age.

Answer Key

Write *(How was prayer a form of worship for the Israelites?)*

Answers will vary. Possible answers: One aspect of the Jewish faith was an active prayer life. The Israelites prayed as a form of worshiping God. They prayed three times a day: in the morning, in the afternoon, and at night. A Jewish prayer book, or siddur, taught the Jewish people how and when to pray. Prayers were split into three categories in the Jewish faith: praising God, giving thanks to God, and asking for help or guidance from God. The Israelites believed that praying brought them closer to God and closer to other Jewish people.

Write *(Explain how Passover is celebrated.)*

Answers will vary. Possible answers: Passover occurs in March or April and lasts for seven or eight days. No one is allowed to work on the first and last two days of the holiday. The beginning of Passover is marked with a very special family meal, called seder. The day before Passover is a fast day to honor Jewish families' firstborn sons who were not killed during the final plague. During Passover, Jewish people do not eat anything made of grains.

Write *(Explain an aspect of Jewish culture.)*

Answers will vary. Possible answers: Jewish people believe that it is through deeds, not faith alone, that the world will be judged, and they learn about good deeds from their religious book, the Torah.

Bat and bar mitzvahs are religious ceremonies followed by a party to honor the boy or girl coming of age in the Jewish faith.

Traditional Jewish people follow strict rules about what they can and cannot eat. For example, meat and dairy products should not be eaten together, people are not allowed to eat pork or shellfish, and foods must be prepared in a particular way to be certain that they are kosher.

Holidays known as High Holy Days' are in September and October. Rosh Hashanah is the Jewish New Year, and Yom Kippur is the ending of the 10-day Rosh Hashanah celebration. Festivals such as Passover are extremely important to Jewish culture as well. Many Jewish people observe the festivals by traveling to the Western Wall for prayer.

Show What You Know

1. False
2. True
3. True
4. False
5. False
6. False
7. True
8. False
9. Answers will vary. Possible answers: Passover is the Jewish holiday that celebrates God sparing the lives of their firstborn sons during the tenth plague of Egypt. Before the Jewish Exodus from Egypt, God passed over them during that same plague. The Jewish people celebrate Passover to commemorate this event.

The Return of the Israelites

Lesson Objectives

By the end of this lesson, your student will be able to:

- trace the developments that occurred when the Israelites entered Canaan
- compare the region of Israel in ancient times with the modern region
- analyze life under the leadership of judges and kings

Supporting Your Student

Read (Israelites in Canaan)

To best support your student through this section, remind them that the process of leaving Egypt and returning to modern-day Israel was long. The Israelites persevered because they believed that Israel was their home, promised to them by God. Have your student underline what occurred upon the Israelites' return to Canaan and number the occurrences to help them process the order of events.

Read (The Region of Israel)

To best support your student through this section, encourage them to look at the maps included before they begin reading. Ask them to explain the difference between the two maps. They should notice that modern-day Israel is smaller and that there are two territories within the borders of Israel that are a different color than the rest of the country. That knowledge will provide the necessary scaffolding for your student to better understand the reading.

Read (The Leadership of Judges versus Kings)

To best support your student through this section, begin by talking to them about different styles of government and how life can be different for people living in a place where the type of government changes or the rulers switch. For example, life was very different for the colonists in the United States when they made the shift from being ruled by the king of England to a president as they became their own country. It was no different for the Israelites.

Learning Styles

Auditory learners may enjoy listening to recordings of the books of the Bible that detail the history of ancient Egypt, such as the book of Judges.

Visual learners may enjoy looking at maps to compare and contrast the region of Israel in ancient and modern times.

Kinesthetic learners may enjoy creating a flowchart to show the transition of the borders of Israel. They could include a map of ancient Israel and modern Israel and note the differences.

Extension Activities

Create a Timeline

Have your student create a timeline to detail the events that took place following the Israelites' return to Canaan through their fall to the Roman Empire. Assist your student in doing research and then allow them to create the timeline digitally or on a piece of poster board.

Create a Presentation

Assist your student in doing research on one of the tribes of Israel, and have them create a presentation (using paper or digitally) to share their knowledge of the tribe they chose.

Answer Key

Write *(Explain what happened when the Israelites entered Canaan.)*

Answers will vary. Possible answers: The Israelites returned to Canaan led by Joshua. Joshua then led the Israelites into battle against the Canaanites and Philistines. During this time, many cities were destroyed, and the Israelites eventually settled into Canaan and led peaceful lives as farmers and herders.

Practice

Answers will vary. Possible answers:

Ancient Israel: area of land that was divided among the 12 tribes of Israel; made up of modern-day Israel, Lebanon, Syria, Palestine, and Jordan; King David centered the civilization around the capital city of Jerusalem

Modern Israel: smaller than it once was; lost land to Syria, Jordan, Lebanon, and Palestine; two territories of Palestine—the West Bank and the Gaza strip—within the borders of Israel that are not governed by the Israelites

Both: same general area

Show What You Know

1. Joshua
2. exiled
3. smaller
4. 12
5. judges
6. David
7. Judah

LESSON 21
Israel's Division and Captivity

Lesson Objectives

By the end of this lesson, your student will be able to:

- identify why the Israelite Kingdom became divided into two kingdoms
- recognize important events that led up to the Israelites' captivity in Babylon
- describe the lives of the Israelites in captivity in Babylon

Supporting Your Student

Explore

The painting in this section depicts the Jews' captivity in Babylon. Assist your student in noticing details about the painting. Examples can be noticing the facial expressions on the people, their body language, what they are wearing, and the landscape in the background. Challenge your student to then make wonder statements based on these findings. For example, your student could write, "I wonder why the man has a shackle on his foot," "I wonder what river they are next to," etc.

Read (Israelite Kingdom Splits)

A common misconception may be the terms used to describe the citizens from the Israelite Kingdom. Once the kingdom splits, people from Israel are sometimes referred to as Samaritans and people from Judah are referred to as Jews. All of the citizens that make up the greater Israelite Kingdom are called Israelites. Therefore, a Samaritan is an Israelite from Israel and a Jew is an Israelite from Judah.

Write (List the events that led up to the Jews' captivity in Babylon.)

Challenge your student to look beyond just dates they may see in the Read section above. While those events with dates listed are important to understanding what led up to the captivity, ask your student to think of why Israelites would be exiled in the first place. Why would the Assyrians or the Chaldeans want to exile an entire population? Is there a reason they would want to keep Jews captive in one place? Point out that exile was used as a form of punishment and control in an empire. Once you and

your student discuss these guiding questions, look for additional events that may have contributed to the Babylon captivity.

Practice

Assist your student in completing the Venn diagram by asking the following guiding questions:

- How was each kingdom formed?
- What were each kingdom's citizens called?
- What empires conquered each kingdom?
- What happened to the Israelites after each kingdom was conquered?
- What happened to the cultural and religious beliefs of each kingdom?
- What leaders did the kingdoms share or not have in common?

Learning Styles

Auditory learners may enjoy writing and giving a speech as an Israelite rebelling against King Rehoboam and asking for less taxes and work requirements.

Visual learners may enjoy drawing their own map of the Israelite Kingdom, Israel, and Judah. They can label cities, bodies of water, and neighboring empires.

Kinesthetic learners may enjoy building a stone temple like Soloman's or a fort to protect Israelites from being conquered by outside empires.

Extension Activities

Biography of a King

With your student, choose a king mentioned in this lesson. Use the internet to research more information about this king. Work with your student to write a short report on the king they chose.

Compare Exiles

With your student, look back on the section about the Samaritans that were scattered and exiled across the Assyrian Empire. What do you think life for those Israelites was like? How was it different from the lives of Jews captive in Babylon? Why weren't the Samaritans able to keep their cultural and religious traditions alive? Why do you think they are called the "ten lost tribes"?

Answer Key

Explore
Answers will vary.

Write (Why did the Israelite Kingdom split into two kingdoms?)
Answers will vary. Possible answers: Israelites were unhappy with the taxes and forced labor Solomon used to build Jerusalem. Some Israelites in the north thought Solomon showed favor to the southern tribes over the northern tribes. Rehoboam became king and Israelites saw this as an opportunity to rebel.

Write (List the events that led up to the Jews' captivity in Babylon.)
Answers will vary. Possible answers: Assyrian and Chaldean empires grew; Assyrians conquered Israel; Assyrians exiled Israelites; Assyrians tried to conquer Judah and failed; Chaldeans conquered Jerusalem; Nebuchadnezzar exiled Judah's king and thousands of Jews; Chaldeans appointed new king in Judah; Jews revolted against Chaldeans and Chaldeans destroyed Jerusalem and exiled remaining Jews

Write (Describe life for the Jews in Babylonian captivity.)
Answers will vary. Possible answers: Jews in Babylon were forced to worship Nebuchadnezzar. They were not allowed to return home to Judah. Some had to change their names. They did not have their leaders or temple. They created synagogues for their community. Rabbis taught the Torah.

Practice
Answers will vary. Possible answers:

Israel: formed from 10 northern tribes of Israelite kingdom; conquered by Assyrians; exiled across Assyrian Empire; lost culture and religion while exiled; weak and disorganized after split; citizens referred to as Samaritans

Judah: formed from two southern tribes of Israelite kingdom; conquered by Chaldeans; exiled to Babylon; kept and strengthened culture and religion while

exiled; strong and independent after split; citizens referred to as Jews

Both: formed from Israelite kingdom; shared kings David and Solomon; citizens referred to as Israelites when part of larger kingdom; practiced Judaism exiled from their homeland

Show What You Know
1.

prophet	someone who shares God's messages and advice
synagogue	a community center for people to gather and practice Judaism
rabbi	a teacher of the Jewish religion and history
exile	to be forced to leave homeland and live in a foreign land

2. Left to right on timeline: B, E, D, A, C

3. B, C, D

4. Answers will vary. Possible answers: Jews created synagogues to be a place to gather and worship together. Rabbis were teachers of the Jewish religion and history. Jews in Babylon stayed together unlike the people from the Kingdom of Israel, who were scattered and unable to stay in a tight community.

Israel Under Greek Rule

Lesson Objectives

By the end of this lesson, your student will be able to:

- identify the events that led to the return of the Jews to Judea
- describe life under the rule of the Greek Empire
- describe the Maccabean Revolt

Supporting Your Student

Read (Jews Return to Judah)

Help your student remember the significance of the Temple of Jerusalem. Ask your student the following guiding questions:

- When was the Temple built?
- What was the effect of Solomon's Temple being built?
- Why was it important for Jews returning to Judah to rebuild this Temple after the Chaldeans destroyed it?

Read (Life Under the Greek Empire)

Make sure your student understands that Judah and Judea refer to the same place. Judah is the name that originated when the Israelite Kingdom split into two separate kingdoms, one named Judah. After the Babylonian Captivity, Jews returned to Judah and eventually changed its name to Judea. From this point forward, Judah was called Judea.

Ask your student if they remember what *diaspora* means. Remind your student that it refers to the scattering of Israelites across the Assyrian Empire and other areas around the world. These are Israelites that were exiled and removed from their homeland. Many exiled Israelites struggle to maintain Jewish culture and religion without their community.

Learning Styles

Auditory learners may enjoy reading aloud some of the Torah that Ezra taught after returning to Judah.

Visual learners may enjoy researching images of the Torah, Greek idols, Antiochus IV, and art from the Maccabean Revolt.

Kinesthetic learners may enjoy building a model of the Temple in Jerusalem.

Extension Activities

Biography

Assist your student in writing a biography about the leader of the Maccabees. Use the internet to research Judas Maccabeus. Take notes on important events. Then write a short biography of this significant Jewish figure.

History of Hanukkah

Assist your student in making connections between the Jewish holiday, Hanukkah, and the results of the Maccabean Revolt. If needed, use the internet to research and learn more information about Hanukkah. Challenge your student to make a multimedia presentation illustrating the history and origins of Hanukkah.

Answer Key

Write *(List three events that led to the Jews' ultimate return to Judah.)*
Answers will vary. Possible answers: The Persian empire conquered the Chaldeans and Babylon, King Cyrus allowed the Jews to return to Judah, Zerubbabel led a group of Jews to Judah, and Ezra led a second group of Jews to Judah.

Write *(How did the lives of Jews change once Antiochus IV became the Greek ruler of Judea?)*
Answers will vary. Possible answers: Jews were not allowed to practice Judaism, Jews were forced to worship Greek gods and goddesses, and Jews were persecuted by Antiochus.

Write *(What caused the Maccabean revolt? What was the effect of the Maccabean revolt?)*
Answers will vary. Possible answers: Jews were persecuted under Greek rule and not allowed to practice Judaism. The Jews also wanted to restore their religion and culture and wanted to get rid of Greek rule. Jews who were against Greek rule worked together to revolt. Because of the revolt, the Second Temple was restored as the center of the Jewish religion. Jews were now leading Judea, and Antiochus and Greek rule left Jerusalem.

Practice
539 BC: B

538 BC: D

458 BC: F

331 BC: G

168 BC: C

167 BC: A

166 BC: H

164 BC: E

Show What You Know
1. uprising
2. Hellenized
3. idols
4. Torah
5. scribes
6. persecuted
7. Answers will vary. Possible answers: The Persian Empire conquers Chaldeans and Babylon, King Cyrus allows Jews to return to Judah, Zerubbabel leads groups of Jews to Judah, and Ezra leads a second group of Jews to Judah.
8. Answers will vary. Possible answers: Greek rulers instead of Jewish leaders, Judaism outlawed, forced to worship Greek gods, persecution, punished or killed for breaking rules
9. False
10. False
11. False
12. True
13. True

Israel Under Roman Rule

Lesson Objectives

By the end of this lesson, your student will be able to:

- describe everyday life in Israel under Roman rule
- describe the destruction of Jerusalem
- describe the fall of Masada

Supporting Your Student

Write *(In what ways was King Herod a tyrant?)*
Support your student by asking the following guiding questions:

- How did King Herod treat the Jews unfairly?
- How was King Herod cruel to the Jews?

Read *(Destruction of Jerusalem)*
Assist your student in understanding the causes of the destruction of Jerusalem. The Romans were already occupying Jerusalem and the Second Temple, so why would they attack and destroy their own city? Why did Jews end up fighting each other during the rebellions? If King Herod built a lavish Second Temple, why would the Romans be willing to destroy it?

Write *(How were the Jews able to continue practicing their religion despite the destruction of Jerusalem and the Temple?)*
Support your student by asking the following guiding questions:

- What did the Jews replace the temple and priests with in order to still practice Judaism?
- How were synagogues and rabbis important during this time?
- How did rabbis teach children the Torah?

Learning Styles

Auditory learners may enjoy watching and listening to videos on the internet about the Jewish revolt against the Romans.

Visual learners may enjoy looking up paintings and drawings of King Herod and Jewish life under Roman control.

Kinesthetic learners may enjoy building a replica of the fortress and Masada.

Extension Activities

Biography
Assist your student in using the internet to research one of the following historical figures from this lesson:

- King Herod
- Rabbi Johanan ben Zakkai
- Flavius Josephus

Your student should then write a short report about the life and importance of this person.

Virtual Field Trip
Assist your student in using the internet to search Masada National Park. Have them watch videos, look at pictures, and read information about Israel's national park. Discuss why this site became a national park and how it compares to national parks in the United States.

Answer Key

Write *(In what ways was King Herod a tyrant?)*
Answers will vary. Possible answers: King Herod was a tyrant because he raised taxes on Jews, spent money on gifts to the Roman emperor, built expensive buildings, did not allow protests, punished Jews who did not like him, and spied on Jews.

Write *(How were Jews able to continue practicing their religion despite the destruction of Jerusalem and the Second Temple?)*
Answers will vary. Possible answers: Synagogues and rabbis replaced the Temple and priests. Synagogues were community centers for Jews to gather, and Rabbis became leaders and taught the Torah. Some rabbis, like Johanan ben Zakkai, formed schools to teach the Torah to children.

Practice
1. Romans take control of Judea.
2. Zealots revolt against Roman rule.
3. Jews take control of Masada.
4. Romans attack Jerusalem.
5. Romans destroy the Second Temple.
6. Jews are exiled from Jerusalem.
7. Some Jews go to Masada for refuge.
8. Romans attack Masada.
9. Jews at Masada die in fire.
10. Romans take back Masada.

Show What You Know
1. D
2. E
3. A
4. B
5. G
6. C
7. F
8. Answers will vary. Possible answers: King Herod was a tyrant because he raised taxes on Jews, spent money on gifts to the Roman Emperor, built expensive buildings, did not allow protests, punished Jews who did not like him, and spied on Jews.

9. Answers will vary. Possible answers: The Romans destroyed Jerusalem and the Second Temple. They were destroyed because the Jews continued to revolt against Roman control. The zealots wanted to fight the Romans.
10. False
11. True
12. False
13. True

Lesson Objectives

By the end of this lesson, your student will review the following big ideas from Chapter 4.

- The culture and religion practiced by the Israelites was called Judaism. (Lessons 18 and 19)
- Ancient Israel was conquered and ruled by many empires, which led to the Jews being in captivity and exiled. (Lessons 20 and 21)
- Life was difficult for Jews as slaves in Egypt, under Greek rule, in Babylonian captivity, and under Roman rule. (Lessons 22 and 23)

Supporting Your Student

Write *(How are modern Jewish religion and culture influenced by the historical events you learned about in this chapter?)*
Support your student by asking the following guiding questions:

- How did the historical events in this chapter influence modern Jewish holidays like Passover and Hanukkah?
- Did events from this chapter strengthen the Jews' belief in Yahweh?
- How did the challenges of the Jews in exile and captivity in Babylon transform Judaism into the modern religion practiced today?
- Modern Judaism still teaches the Torah. How did these historical events influence the writings in these books?
- How are ruins from the destruction of buildings during battles important to Jews today?

Practice *(Timeline)*
Assist your student in choosing their six events for the timeline. Discuss with your student why they chose the events they did. How did they determine which events were most important? Challenge your student to determine whether one event caused another. Ask your student to figure out the amount of time between each event.

Practice *(Cause and Effect)*
Support your student by asking the following guiding questions:

- Why do you think only some of the Israelites thought Solomon's taxes and labor were unfair?
- What happened when Israelites were divided on their opinions of Solomon's kingdom?
- How did the Jews end up away from their homes and in a foreign land?
- Who was the leader of the Jews before Babylonian captivity?
- What empire had recently conquered Judah before Babylonian captivity?
- Why did the Jews and the Maccabees want to force the Greeks out of Jerusalem?
- Who was the Greek ruler at that time? Did the Jewish people like him?
- How were Jews oppressed under King Herod and the Romans?
- What happened after the zealots rebelled?

Learning Styles

Auditory learners may enjoy watching and listening to a documentary or video about ancient Israel.

Visual learners may enjoy drawing pictures depicting events throughout ancient Israel's history.

Kinesthetic learners may enjoy acting out different events from ancient Israel's history.

Extension Activities

Write a Short Story
Have your student choose one historical event from ancient Israel's history. They should create characters and a plot line for their story. The story should take place during the historical event. When your student is finished writing their story, ask them to read it aloud.

Travel Brochure
Imagine traveling to Israel today. What historical sites would be important to visit? Have your student research tourist sites in Israel using the internet.

Then have them make a travel brochure advertising places to visit while on a vacation in Israel. Have them include pictures (drawings or photos printed from the internet) and reasons why these places are historically significant. When your student is finished, ask them to present their brochure.

Answer Key

Write *(How are modern Jewish religion and culture influenced by the historical events you learned about in this chapter?)*

Answers will vary. Possible answers: Holidays like Passover and Hanukkah were created to celebrate or remember events we learned about in this chapter like the exodus from Egypt or the rededication of the Temple after the Maccabees defeated the Greek armies.

Jews' belief in monotheism, or one god, Yahweh, was tested when the Greeks were in control and forced Jews to worship Greek gods and goddesses.

Despite being in captivity in Babylon and exiled from Jerusalem, Jews adapted and kept their religion strong.

Stories in the Torah and Hebrew Bible were accounts of events that happened during this time period.

Many Jews visit the Western Wall or Masada National Park when visiting Israel because these are significant sites in their religion and are the result of events that happened in this chapter.

Rabbis and synagogues were created out of necessity when Jews were in exile; these are still important today in Judaism.

Practice *(Vocabulary)*

- Torah: the first five books of Jewish scriptures, the Jewish law
- synagogue: a Jewish place of worship, a community center for people to gather and practice Judaism
- zealot: a person who will fight for their ideas, religion, and freedom
- exile: to be forced to leave one's homeland and live in a foreign land
- Hellenized: to become Greek and go along with Greek culture
- scroll: a long piece of parchment paper used for writing
- rabbi: a teacher of the Jewish religion and history
- conquer: to defeat and successfully overcome
- empire: a group of nations ruled by one leader

Practice *(Timeline)*

Your student may choose any six events from this chapter. Below is a list of all events covered in the chapter and their corresponding years:

- The Israelites left Egypt to return to Canaan in 1300 BC.
- The Israelites went into battle against the Canaanites and Philistines for their land, Canaan, in 1100 BC.
- The Israelite Kingdom split into Judah and Israel in 928 BC.
- The Assyrian Empire conquered Israel and exiled Samaritans in 722 BC.
- The Chaldeans conquered Judah, and the Temple was destroyed in 597 BC.
- The Jews revolted against Chaldean rule and were exiled to Babylon in 586 BC.
- The Persian king in Babylon allowed the Jews to return to Judah in 538 BC.
- Alexander the Great conquered Judah and began Greek rule in 331 BC.
- Greek ruler Antiochus outlawed Judaism and persecuted the Jews in 168 BC.
- The Maccabees took back Jerusalem in 164 BC.
- The Romans conquered Judah in 63 BC.
- The Jews revolted against King Herod and Roman rule in AD 66.
- Jerusalem and the Temple were destroyed, and the Jews were exiled in AD 70.
- The fall of Masada happened, and no Jews were left in Judah in AD 73.

Practice *(Cause and Effect)*

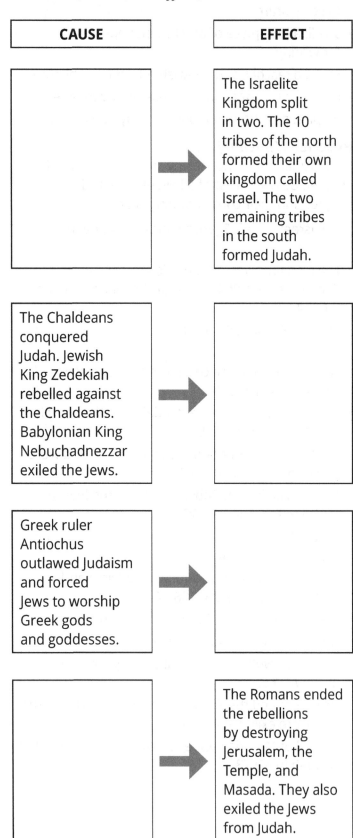

CAUSE	EFFECT
	The Israelite Kingdom split in two. The 10 tribes of the north formed their own kingdom called Israel. The two remaining tribes in the south formed Judah.
The Chaldeans conquered Judah. Jewish King Zedekiah rebelled against the Chaldeans. Babylonian King Nebuchadnezzar exiled the Jews.	
Greek ruler Antiochus outlawed Judaism and forced Jews to worship Greek gods and goddesses.	
	The Romans ended the rebellions by destroying Jerusalem, the Temple, and Masada. They also exiled the Jews from Judah.

Quick Review

Refer to the statement your student circled in the Show What You Know section to self-assess their knowledge of the chapter concepts. Then to assist in determining if your student is ready to take the assessment, consider:

- Having your student summarize the history of ancient Israel by reciting the order of events and which empires were in control of Israel in what order.

- Having your student describe the culture and religion of the Jewish people by talking about specific holidays, Yahweh, the Torah, the Tabernacle, rabbis, synagogues, and specific traditions.

- Having your student describe what life was like for the Jews in Egypt, under Greek rule, in Babylonian captivity, and under Roman rule.

Discover! SOCIAL STUDIES • GRADE 6 • CHAPTER 4 ASSESSMENT

73

Chapter Assessment

Fill in the blanks using the vocabulary words in the word bank below.

Word Bank: Torah   exiled   rabbi   synagogue   persecuted   zealot   Canaan

1. A Jewish _____ was a person willing to fight for their beliefs and freedom.

2. A scribe named Ezra wrote the first five books of the _____ onto scrolls after returning to Judah from Babylon.

3. _____ refers to the land that makes up modern-day Israel and that ancient Israelites believed was given to them by Yahweh.

4. Samaritans from Israel were _____, or forced to leave their home, and scattered across the Assyrian Empire.

5. During exile and captivity, the _____ was an important figure in keeping Judaism alive because they taught the Torah.

6. Greek rulers, like Antiochus, _____ Jews and treated them unfairly because of their religion.

7. A _____ is a Jewish community center and place for worship.

8. Describe some of the challenges and difficulties of the Jewish people during this time period.

   ....

   ....

   ....

Order the events from 1 to 5. Write the number on the blank next to each event.

9. _____ The Israelite Kingdom splits in two.

10. _____ Judaism is outlawed, and Jews are forced to worship Greek gods.

11. _____ Israelites leave Egypt to return to Canaan.

12. _____ Jews are exiled and held captive in Babylon.

13. _____ Romans destroy Jerusalem and the Temple.

Chapter Assessment Answer Key

1. zealot
2. Torah
3. Canaan
4. exiled
5. rabbi
6. persecuted
7. synagogue
8. Answers will vary. Possible answers:
   - Israelites were forced to leave Canaan and go to Egypt because of a famine.
   - Israelites became slaves in Egypt.
   - Israelites wandered the desert for 40 years during the Exodus.
   - The Israelite Kingdom split into Israel and Judah.
   - Both Israel and Judah were conquered by other empires.
   - Jews tried to revolt against the Chaldeans and ended up exiled and in captivity in Babylon.
   - Under Greek rule, Judaism was outlawed, and Jews were forced to worship Greek gods.
   - Under Roman rule, Jews were oppressed, and when they rebelled, Jerusalem and the Temple were destroyed. Jews were exiled from Judah.
9. 2
10. 4
11. 1
12. 3
13. 5

Alternative Assessment

Project: Poster Timeline

Project Requirements and Steps:

1. You will need a piece of poster board, markers, tape or glue, scissors, and printer paper.

2. You will make a timeline on your poster to include all dates discussed in Chapter 4.

3. Review each lesson and take notes of any events and dates.

4. Once you have your list of events and dates, plan how you will organize your timeline on the poster board.

5. Create a vertical or horizontal timeline, making sure each event is in order, has the correct date, and includes a description of the event.

6. Draw or print pictures from the internet to include on your poster. Make sure to write a short caption for each picture.

7. Create a title for your timeline.

8. Be creative and clear in your presentation.

9. When you are finished, share your poster with your instructor.

Alternative Assessment Rubric

Use the following rubric to grade your student's assessment.

					Points
Title	The timeline has a creative and effective title.	The timeline has an effective title.	The timeline has a title.	The title is missing or difficult to read or locate.	
Documentation of Events	The timeline contains all significant events. This includes dates and descriptions.	The timeline contains most events. The date is included. The description is basic.	The timeline contains some events. A few dates and descriptions are missing.	Most events, dates, and descriptions are missing.	
Accuracy	All events, dates, and descriptions are detailed and accurate.	All events, dates, and descriptions are accurate.	Some events, dates, and descriptions are accurate.	Many events, dates, and descriptions are not accurate.	
Appearance	The poster is attractive, creative, and organized.	The poster is organized and shows some creativity.	The poster is organized but lacks creativity.	The poster is not organized or creative.	
Drawings or Pictures	Great pictures and drawings that are organized and balanced with events are included. Specific captions are included.	Relevant pictures and drawings with captions are included.	Few pictures and drawings are included, or the pictures and drawings are not relevant. No captions are included.	No pictures, drawings, or captions are included.	

Total Points _____/20

Average _____

Lesson Objectives

By the end of this lesson, your student will be able to:

- locate ancient and modern places in India and the surrounding countries on a map
- identify key features of ancient Indian homes
- identify evidence that the Harappan civilization was highly advanced
- identify possible reasons why the Harappan civilization disappeared

Supporting Your Student

Read (*The Ancient People of the Indus Valley*)
It is important to understand that many ancient civilizations started out as nomads and lived in small family groups until they were able to grow enough food to feed large amounts of people. The ground in the Indus River Valley was a lot like that in the Fertile Crescent and the Nile River Valley. The rivers would routinely flood and then recede, leaving behind extremely fertile silt. The people of this area learned how to grow large amounts of cereal crops, so only a few of the people had to work as farmers. The rest of the people learned how to do other skills, like planning and building a city, raising animals, mining, or creating crafts for trading.

To help your student understand the concept of urban planning, you could reference how modern cities are constructed and compare them to Harappan cities. Most cities have a large downtown area surrounded by residential areas. The Harappans built their citadel, public bath, and grainery in the downtown area of their city, while the majority of the people lived in neighborhoods around and below these public spaces. Then you could ask your student guiding questions, such as, "Why is it useful to have a specified public space, like a downtown area, that is separate from residential areas? How would the creation of a downtown public space have benefitted Harappans?"

Another aspect of urban planning is the use of pipes and sewage systems to bring fresh water into the city and take waste out. Ask guiding questions to expand on this concept, such as, "How are pipes and sewage systems indicators of good urban design? How would these systems help the Harappans live comfortably within their cities? How do these designs compare to those of other ancient civilizations, like Mesopotamia and Egypt?"

Read (*Harappan Growth and Disappearance*)
Remnants of the Harappan civilization have been found throughout Mesopotamia, so historians know that trade was a major part of the Harappan culture. It would be good to examine a map of the Middle East and Asia to show that the Indus River Valley would have been a good stopping point for those traders moving between Mesopotamia and China. If you can, view a resource like Google Maps or a topographical map so that your student can explore the terrain of that area and talk about what it may have been like for the traders of that time period. Point out significant geographical information:

- The Indus River Valley was a floodplain, similar to the area of the Fertile Crescent and the Nile. This means that the area had good farmland that allowed the Harappans to grow enough food for everyone in the cities.
- It is located just beyond several mountain ranges, so it would have been a good place for travelers to stop for food and water after a hard trek.
- The Harappan harbors would have been the best place for merchants to stop on their way from Mesopotamia before having to travel around the Indian peninsula. Also, it may have been easier to bring goods up the river toward China instead of trying to sail so far.

When discussing the disappearance of the Harappan civilization, explain that, unlike some of the other civilizations (mainly those in Mesopotamia and Egypt), there has not been any evidence found that the Harappan civilization was dispersed due to war or any type of human violence. As far as historians can tell, the Harappans dispersed voluntarily, but they do not really know why. They do know that the Sarasvati River (the main river that flowed past the city of Harappa) started to dry up around the time the people started to disperse. Also, the Aryan people did move into the Indus River Valley, but it has been shown that their arrival was mostly peaceful, and it is possible that the Harappans chose to adopt many aspects of the Aryan culture. This is important information to discuss because it illustrates how changes in geography or culture can impact human decisions. If they were no longer able to grow enough food because the river dried up, they would not have been able to live in their cities.

Write *(What parts of the Harappan culture show that they were a technologically advanced civilization for their time period?)*

Some parts of this answer may be obvious to your student, such as having toilets and wells within their homes, but some other things to discuss would be the strengths in urban design shown by the Harappans. Setting up their cities so that homes were easily accessible but still separated from the main streets meant that the people were able to live relatively peaceful lives within a very crowded city. Also, the fact that almost every home had access to fresh water and a sewer system meant that they planned these systems to be able to handle the growth that typically happens in cities.

Learning Styles

Auditory learners may enjoy listening to an audiobook about ancient history and, more specifically, the Harappan civilization. A great option is *The Story of the World* by Susan Wise Bauer. They may also enjoy discussing the different things that they have learned about the different ancient civilizations.

Visual learners may enjoy watching the videos about the Indus Valley Civilization created by the World History Encyclopedia. Search "Indus Valley Civilization" for examples.

Kinesthetic learners may enjoy planning and creating a structure from a Harappan city, such as a house or The Great Bath, using crafting materials, such as modeling clay. This will help your student get a better idea of Harappan urban design.

Extension Activities

Field Trip

To help your student understand urban design, it may be helpful to take them for a walk in a nearby city so they can explore how the different systems work together. For example, you can show them how main roads are often larger than those that go through residential neighborhoods, and how various systems (like electrical and sewer) run under the roads that we use. You could discuss how the Harappan cities and modern cities are similar or different.

Map

To help your student visualize the area inhabited by the Harappan people, have them create a three-dimensional map of the region on a large piece of cardboard. They can use a topographical map as a reference and build up areas with mountains with salt dough (two cups of flour, one cup of salt, and one cup of cold water mixed together). Then they can paint areas with craft paint and label the important bodies of water, Harappan cities, and landforms. If you want them to get even more in-depth, you could have them include Mesopotamia and indicate the trade routes that the ancient peoples used to travel.

Answer Key

Write *(How does your home compare to a Harappan home?)*

Answers will vary. Possible answers: Their home has a water source, windows, and a bathroom. Their house may not have a flat roof or a courtyard, but they may have a backyard, patio, or deck that serves a similar purpose to a courtyard.

Write *(What parts of the Harappan culture show that they were a technologically advanced civilization?)*

Answers will vary, but should include something about the Harappan civilization having homes with wells, toilets, and a form of air-conditioning; a complex water and sewer system throughout the city; and excellent urban design, such as wide roads and homes clustered into neighborhoods.

Practice

1. Mohenjo Daro

2. bath

3. Harappa

4. urban design

5. courtyard

6. lapis lazuli

7. Mesopotamia

8. toilet

9. Indus River

10. citadel

Show What You Know

1. B

2. A

3. A, B, C

4. B

5. A

6. C

7. Answers will vary. Possible answer: One hypothesis is that they left because the rivers they lived near dried up. This would make sense because they would not be able to grow enough food and would need to move to a place where they could.

Lesson Objectives

By the end of this lesson, your student will be able to:

- identify characteristics of the Aryan civilization
- describe the principles of Hinduism
- explain how a person's caste affected their relationships and choices in life
- analyze the benefits or disadvantages of the caste system for members of different castes

Supporting Your Student

Explore

When talking to your student about their culture, make sure to talk about things like language, food, and religion. Then see if you can help your student dive deeper into their culture. Consider the following:

- Living situations (nuclear family vs. extended family)
- Clothing choices
- Music and visual/performing arts
- Manners and social interactions

One way to really help your student delve into this topic is to have them research another country with a very different culture than their own. What do they notice about that country's culture? Then have them reverse it and pretend to be someone from another place visiting your home. This role reversal will help them notice the everyday things that they take for granted.

Read (The Aryan Civilization)

While reading this section, it would be a great idea to research the assumed pathways of the Aryans when they migrated down into India. A wonderful resource is an online map or Earth model that shows the terrain of that area. They can zoom in and out to get an idea of just how far those people traveled to get to India. You could also discuss with your student the difficulty the Aryans may have faced on their journey.

Another great idea is to look at the physical differences between northern Indians and southern Indians. Northern Indians tend to be slightly taller and have lighter skin than their southern counterparts. This is a way for your student to visualize how the arrival of the Aryans impacted the native Indian population.

Read (The Caste System)

The Hindu caste system consists of four different groups:

1. Brahmin: The first caste was made up of intellectuals and priests. These were considered the most important people, and they usually had the nicest homes and the best food. They were typically vegetarians because they wanted to avoid hurting other life forms and because they considered a vegetarian diet purifying to the body and mind.

2. Kshatriya (Sha-tree-uh): The second caste consisted of warriors and governing officials. These people were also some of the most important in Hindu society, but they were one step below the priests and academics. These were the people that would fight battles and develop laws for the rest of the people. The Kshatriyas and the Brahmins would often work together to govern the people and would get along well with one another, but they were not allowed to marry one another or leave their caste.

3. Vaishya (Vi-she-ah): The third caste was made up of farmers, crafters, and other skilled laborers. These people rarely interacted with those of the two upper castes unless they had business to discuss. They usually had decent homes to live in and plenty of food to eat. The majority of people continued working in the same career field as their parents. For example, a child born to painters grew up to be a painter.

4. Shudra (Shoo-drah): The fourth caste was made up of the servant class. These were the people that did the unskilled labor for the other three classes. They were often paid very poorly, and they were not allowed to go to school. They did not always have a nice home or enough to eat, but they were allowed to participate in society.

5. Dalit (Da-luht): These were the "Untouchables" in Hindu society, and they did not belong to the caste system at all. It was much better to be a Shudra than a Dalit. These people had to take the worst jobs of society, and they were not allowed to interact with anyone from other castes.

To help your student better understand the castes, you could work together to name different professions and then see if they can figure out which caste they would belong to. For example, a soldier would belong to the Kshatriya caste, while a waiter would belong to the Shudra class. Make sure to emphasize that this is a system that is no longer in use and that sorting professions just helps to apply the caste system to something that is already understood. This sorting does not mean that someone who works as a soldier is somehow better than someone who works as a waiter.

It may also help your student explore the caste system more deeply by discussing the following:

- How did the caste system help society? It ensured that there were always people to do every job required, even the jobs that no one wanted to do.
- How did the caste system hurt society? It placed people in positions they are not skilled enough to do. For example, someone born in the Kshatriya caste that was not a talented warrior or governing official could have caused a great amount of harm filling that role.

Learning Styles

Auditory learners may enjoy discussing the Aryan migration and how it impacted the local people that were already living in India.

Visual learners may enjoy creating a graphic organizer that helps them organize the different castes of Hinduism.

Kinesthetic learners may enjoy drawing a map that shows the Aryan migration into modern-day India.

Extension Activities

Create a Poster
Have your student create a poster that explains the core beliefs of Hinduism. They should include the following:

- The cycle of death and rebirth
- The names of the different gods and their roles
- The terms samsara, dharma, karma, and moksha and what they mean
- The caste system as it relates to Hinduism

Create a 3-D Caste Model
Have your student design and build a three-dimensional model that can be used to represent the castes of Hinduism. They could use cardboard, building blocks, wood, or any other type of material to build their model. They can use figurines to represent people, or they can create symbols for each of the different castes. They should make sure to put the castes in the correct order, and the symbols should be easy to match with the caste they are meant to represent.

Answer Key

Explore
Answers will vary depending on your student's culture. The answer should include something about religion, food, social interactions, language, arts, and clothing.

Write *(The Aryan people changed from a nomadic lifestyle to a settled one. Which style of living do you think is better? Why?)*
Answers will vary based on your student's opinion. They should back up their opinion with information from either the text or prior knowledge.

Write *(Think about the jobs your parents have. How would you feel if you knew that you would have to do that job too?)*

Answers will vary.

Practice

1. Kshatriya
2. Dalit
3. Vaishya
4. Brahmin
5. Shudra

Show What You Know

1. nomads
2. Vedas
3. karma
4. D
5. C
6. B
7. E
8. A
9. Answers will vary. Possible answers: A person's caste determined the work they were allowed to do. People from lower castes were not allowed to speak to people of upper castes. People were not able to marry outside of their castes.

Buddhism in Ancient India

Lesson Objectives

By the end of this lesson, your student will be able to:

- trace Siddhartha Gautama's development of Buddhism
- explain why many people in the lower castes and untouchables were drawn to Buddhism
- compare Buddhist beliefs with Christianity and Hinduism

Supporting Your Student

Explore

It would be a good idea to talk to your student about some of the different holidays and traditions that your family participates in that are attached to your culture or beliefs. Try to steer them away from things that are not highly meaningful to your family, such as a holiday that your family observes but does not connect with your family's core beliefs or morals.

Write *(Why do you think it would be easier for someone from a lower caste to convert to Buddhism and harder for someone in a higher caste?)*

Have your student focus on what Siddhartha Gautama did to become the Buddha. He gave up his life in a beautiful palace, where he was always comfortable and well-fed, to live the life of a monk who spent most of his time meditating. He gave up all of his worldly possessions and power, and that led him to enlightenment. That type of sacrifice can seem difficult to people who have a lot of things and enjoy a lot of social standing and power.

Read *(Buddhism, Hinduism, and Christianity)*

Along with what is written in the text, you could also talk about:

- How both Jesus and the Buddha taught the importance of not being attached to worldly goods.
- Buddhism and Christianity originated with a single teacher (the Buddha and Jesus Christ), while Hinduism did not.
- Buddhism and HInduism are extremely individualistic, where believers focus on improving themselves and living to meet the ideals of their

faith. Christianity, however, teaches that, while one should live a Christ-like life, it is the mission of Christians to spread the Gospel of Jesus Christ and their salvation does not come from good works alone.

Practice

Ensure that your student knows how to fill out a Venn diagram. Characteristics that are unique to a faith should be put on the part of each circle that does not overlap the others. Those characteristics that are shared should be put in the area of the circles that overlap.

Learning Styles

Auditory learners may enjoy listening to audio retellings of various Buddhist fables called Jataka tales.

Visual learners may enjoy looking at traditional Buddhist art, such as Tibetan mandalas, and learning about why Buddhists participate in these art forms.

Kinesthetic learners may enjoy doing some of the activities associated with Buddhism and Hinduism, such as meditation and yoga. These do not need to be done as a religious activity but as a way to understand why Buddhists and Hindus do these activities to help them live better lives.

Extension Activities

Field Trip

If you live in an area where this is possible, take a field trip to an art museum and go to the different areas that show Buddhist, Hindu, and Christian artwork. Talk to your student about what they see in the artwork and how it relates to the beliefs of each religion.

Eightfold Path Wheel Collage

Have your student research the Eightfold Path and create a wheel that shows each part. Then have them find pictures that illustrate each part of the path and paste them into the proper sections of the wheel.

Below are the steps of the Eightfold Path and some picture ideas:

1. **Right View** (actions have consequences or karma)—endless knot to show cycle of cause and effect

2. **Right Intention** (living a life of loving kindness and compassion)—person showing compassion or kindness to another living creature or person

3. **Right Speech** (no lying, rude speech, or gossip)—words that show truth and kindness

4. **Right Action** (no killing or injuring)—people holding hands and being kind

5. **Right Livelihood** (only doing work that sustains life)—jobs that help people, like a doctor

6. **Right Effort** (maintain a joyful attitude)—someone doing work with a joyful attitude

7. **Right Mindfulness** (be in the moment)—someone enjoying a moment in nature or while creating

8. **Right Concentration** (focusing on a worthy object or thought)—someone meditating

Go over the different spokes with your student when they are finished.

Answer Key

Explore
Answers will vary depending on which holiday or tradition your family observes.

Write *(Why do you think it would be easier for someone from a lower caste to convert to Buddhism and harder for someone in a higher caste?)*
Answers will vary. Possible answers: People of the higher castes struggled with Buddhism because they were required to give up their worldly goods and social statuses. Buddhists did not believe in the caste system and maintained that all people were of equal worth. People from a lower caste did not have as many worldly goods to give up and would enjoy a better social standing if they were seen to have equal worth.

Practice
Answers will vary. Possible answers:

Hinduism: maintains a caste system where one's social standing depends on birth and karma; polytheistic, believers worship different gods like Shiva, Brahma, and Vishnu

Christianity: monotheistic, believes that there is one God; Bible is the spiritual text; founded by Jesus Christ, who they believe is the son of God

Buddhism: focuses on individual improvement and does not give any special attention to God; spend time meditating on the Four Noble Truths and the Eightfold Path; founded by the Buddha

Show What You Know

1. A
2. C
3. B
4. D
5. B
6. Answers will vary. Possible answer: Buddhism was appealing to the people of the lower castes and untouchables because it rejected the caste system and taught that all people were of equal worth.
7. B
8. C
9. A

Lesson Objectives

By the end of this lesson, your student will be able to:

- describe Sanskrit's influence on English
- compare and contrast Sanskrit and English
- describe the importance of language in ancient India

Supporting Your Student

Explore

If your student is unsure about what word to research, try to give them ideas for very basic words. Try to guide them toward uncomplicated words that may have an intense etymology. Some good words for them to research are *spoon*, *shoes*, *refrigerator*, and *flower*. Let them look at a few different words before choosing one to use for their assignment.

Read *(The Ancient Languages of India)*

Review the Hindu castes with your student so that they understand why the people of the Brahmin caste are the only ones that still speak Sanskrit. Here is a quick overview:

1. Brahmins—These are the teachers and spiritual leaders in Hindu society. They use Sanskrit while studying the Vedas and while performing religious ceremonies.

2. Kshatriyas—The governing caste and warriors use some Sanskrit when performing matters of state because Sanskrit is still used in some small regions of India.

3. Vaishyas—People in this caste include merchants, farmers, and skilled laborers. They may use Sanskrit if they live in one of the few regions where it is still used, but they wouldn't use it much.

4. Shudras—The servant class would not use Sanskrit much, if at all, because they are not educated.

5. Dalits—The Untouchables would not speak Sanskrit because it is considered a holy language, and it would be socially unacceptable for them to use it.

Read *(Sanskrit vs. English)*

To help your student understand the connection between English and the other Indo-European languages, write down the following words on a whiteboard or piece of paper. They will show the similarities between Sanskrit and Latin/Germanic-based languages.

Root Sanskrit Word	Latin/Greek/ Germanic Word	English Word
gau (g-ow)	cū (Germanic - Old English)	cow
naama	nomen (Latin)/ nama (Germanic)	name
patha (way)	pathes(Greek)/ pæth (Germanic)	path
sunu (offspring)	sunu (Germanic)	son
lubh (to care)	lubo (Latin and Germanic)	love

Discuss how the words are similar to each other and how this may have helped historians connect these languages to one very ancient language that influenced all of them.

Learning Styles

Auditory learners may enjoy listening to native speakers say different words in Sanskrit and other Indo-European languages (French, Hindi, Polish, etc.). Hearing how the words are pronounced will help them notice similarities and differences. Find video or audio of native speakers online.

Visual learners may enjoy creating images that connect the different languages. For example, they could draw a cow and write the different Indo-European words for *cow*. Make sure they include Sanskrit.

Kinesthetic learners may enjoy using index cards and string to create a large diagram connecting the Indo-European languages, similar to the one found in their text.

Extension Activities

Catalog an Artifact

To help your student understand how archeologists and historians find out information about different cultures, create a "dig site" in your backyard or inside a large container. You can use dirt, sand, or even rice as your substrate and then bury different "artifacts." These could be fake jewelry, coins, small tools, and pieces of paper with writing on them. Have your student use string to section out the dig site and carefully search for artifacts. When they find one, they should catalog where they found it, what it is, and what they think it may have been used for. They should also come up with other inferences about the "civilization" they are exploring. For example, if they find a coin, they can assume that the culture used money or some sort of bartering system and that they had some sort of social hierarchy (usually only important people get put on coins).

Sanskrit Name

Do an online search for "how to write my name in Sanskrit." Have your student figure out what their name in Sanskrit looks like, and then have them try rewriting it on paper and decorating their name. They can put this up on their bedroom door or use it to decorate their room.

Answer Key

Explore

Your student's etymology diagram should go back to one of the ancient languages (even if not an Indo-European language). They should not choose words that have been recently added to the English language. Ask your student if they found anything that was interesting when they looked up the word.

Write (Why do you think only members of the upper castes are taught Sanskrit?)

Answers will vary. Possible answers: Only people in the upper castes are educated, and Sanskrit is the holy language of Hinduism. It makes sense that only the Brahmin caste would learn it because they are the priests and teachers of Hinduism.

Answers will vary. Possible answers:

- There may have been so many variations because people tended to live in isolated tribes in India until the arrival of the Aryans. This would cause each group of people to develop their own language.
- There may have been so many variations because the people of the lower castes were not taught Sanskrit, so they would have had to have their own language in order to communicate.

Write (Why do you think it may be easier to learn how to read Sanskrit than it would be to learn English?)

Answers will vary. Possible answers: Sanskrit has different letters for each sound, so while it would take longer to remember all the letters, you would not have to remember all the different sounds one letter can make like you do with English. Also, you would not have to figure out which sound that letter makes in each word when reading.

Practice

The words and phrases should be written in the following places.

Sanskrit: 52 letters, ancient language, holy language, Indo-Iranian origin, mostly unchanged, different letter for each sound

Both: phonetic, Indo-European language

English: 26 letters, young language, used worldwide, Germanic origin, constantly changing, letters make different sounds depending on use

Show What You Know

1. B

2. A

3. C

4. A

5. B

6. B

7. Answers will vary. Possible answers: Sanskrit has not changed much because it is considered a holy language of the Hindu religion. Also, it is not used much today except for in a few areas of India, so it would not have evolved as much as English.

Lesson Objectives

By the end of this lesson, your student will be able to:

- describe the important events that led to the creation of the Mauryan Empire
- distinguish between positive and negative aspects of Chandragupta Maurya's rule
- identify reasons that many people think Ashoka is the most important Mauryan ruler

Supporting Your Student

Explore

This would be a great time to review some of the great empires that your student has learned about, like Egypt and Mesopotamia. Some great rulers brought those kingdoms together, such as King Narmer, who combined Upper and Lower Egypt, and Hammurabi, who created the Babylonian Empire.

Work with your student to do some short research on one or two of these leaders so they have a base to compare to the Mauryan Empire, and discuss with your student some of the qualities and personality traits that these people shared that made them effective leaders. Ask your student to identify events and situations that allowed these people to gain power.

Read (The Path to the Mauryans)

Review some of what your student learned in prior lessons. This will help them understand how the prior events led to the transition from the Nanda Dynasty to the Mauryans. Here are good topics for review:

- Hindu caste system and the Vedas—Go through the different castes and remind your student that the Vedas were the sacred texts of Hinduism. Castes are Brahmin (priests), Kshatriya (warriors/leaders), Vaishya (merchants and skilled workers), Shudra (unskilled labor and servants), and Dalit (Untouchables).
- Indus River Valley (IRV) civilization—How are they similar to and different from the ancient Kingdoms like Magadha and Maurya?

- Similarities include organized government that controlled a lot of land.
- Differences include no indication of a king or ruler or of the IRV civilization making much of an attempt to gain new territory. They were more concerned with maintaining trade.

Emphasize the importance of each event in history. For example, if Dhana Nanda had not dismissed Chanakya, then Chanakya would not have had a reason to go to Chandragupta Maurya, and the Mauryan Empire might never have existed.

Read (Chandragupta Maurya)

Most of what we know about the first ruler of the Mauryan Empire we have learned from legends and folklore, and each story is different depending on who is telling it. Many historians believe that he originally came from a Kshatriya family that had fallen on hard times, so he grew up among members of the Vaishya caste and had a humble start to life. Regardless of where he came from, Chandragupta was ambitious and had a goal of gaining power and authority. His background as part of the Kshatriya caste may have made him more desirable than Dhana Nanda, who historians think came from a Shudra background.

- Use the above information and your review of the castes to talk to your student about why Chandragupta was a more desirable leader than Dhana Nanda.
- A good way to present this information is by using the caste pyramid. Write Chandragupta's name in the Kshatriya spot (second from stop) and Dhana Nanda in the Shudra spot (fourth spot). In the Hindu society, Chandragupta's birth position would have been seen as greater than Nanda's and his rule ordained by the gods.

Read (Ashoka the Great)

Ashoka was a popular ruler, and not just because he conquered lots of land. Review with your student what it means to be Buddhist and how that would help Ashoka connect with the people of ancient India.

- Remember that Buddhism does not support the caste system, so Ashoka would have been accepted by the members of Hindu upper castes because of his high-born status, but his Buddhist policies would have appealed to people of the lower castes.

Learning Styles

Auditory learners may enjoy listening to a podcast about the ancient Mauryan Empire so they can hear other scholars talk about Ashoka.

Visual learners may enjoy drawing out maps to show the spread of the Magadha kingdom and the Mauryan Empire. Split the Mauryan Empire into the territories gained by Chandragupta, Bindusara, and Ashoka. This will help them visualize how each leader expanded their territory.

Kinesthetic learners may enjoy building a life-size timeline with index cards and string. They can start with the Indus River Valley civilization and add information from their reading, going up to the rule of Ashoka. This will help them remember dates and the order of events.

Extension Activities

Create a Poster

Have your student choose one of the figures from their lesson to research. Then they should create a poster that includes the figure's estimated birth and death, maps of their empire or kingdom, and any of their major accomplishments.

Play a Game

Play a game like Risk to help your student understand the different ways that empires are created.

Virtual Field Trip

Help your student search online for "virtual tour of the Mauryan Empire" and explore the various art pieces and historical sites you find. Look at stupas and the Ashokan pillars that were built during Ashoka's reign and help your student research more about why they were built.

Answer Key

Write (How was the caste system important in the establishment of rulers and kingdoms?)
Answers will vary. Possible answers: The caste system placed people in a social hierarchy. Before the Aryans arrived, the people lived with a government that did not have a single ruler. The caste system made it so that people expected rulers to come from the Kshatriya caste, so there were many who did not recognize Dhana Nanda because it was believed he was from the Shudra caste.

Write (How would you describe Chandragupta to someone who knew nothing about him?)
Answers will vary. Possible answers: Chandragupta was ambitious and persistent. He was a ruler who worked hard to expand his empire to include most of ancient India.

Write (Why do you think Ashoka was called Ashoka the Great?)
Answers will vary. Possible answers: He was called Ashoka the Great because he conquered the kingdom of Kalinga, but then he realized that war was destructive. He decided to stop going to war and concentrate on improving the lives of the people of his empire.

Show What You Know

1. A

2. C

3. C

4. B

5. A

6. A. 6
   B. 2
   C. 7
   D. 4
   E. 3
   F. 1
   G. 5

7. Answers will vary. Possible answers: After becoming a Buddhist, Ashoka stopped going to war and focused on improving the lives of his citizens, creating laws that benefited all the people of his kingdom, and sent Buddhist missionaries to other countries.

Lesson Objectives

By the end of this lesson, your student will review the following big ideas from Chapter 5.

- The Harappans lived in the Indus River Valley and created technologically advanced homes and cities. For unknown reasons, they left their cities and moved further east. (Lesson 25)
- The Aryan civilization migrated into India and introduced Hinduism and the caste system. These are both large parts of Indian society today. (Lesson 26)
- After extensive study, Siddhartha Gautama developed a faith called Buddhism that teaches self-discipline as a way to reach enlightenment. Buddhism does not uphold the Hindu caste system, so it drew in many members of the lower castes. (Lesson 27)
- Sanskrit is one of the oldest languages in the world and originated with the Aryans. It is the holy language of Hinduism. It has some similarities to English because they both originated from the Indo-European language family. (Lesson 28)
- The Mauryan Empire was established by Chandragupta Maurya, and his grandson, Ashoka, is considered one of the greatest leaders of ancient India because of his ability to lead with passion, wisdom, and sensitivity to his people. (Lesson 29)

Supporting Your Student

Review (Ancient Indian Culture)
While reading through this section, encourage your student to stop and verbally summarize some important facts that were highlighted. When they have read each section, encourage them to go back and highlight any vocabulary words they might have seen. This will help them remember their vocabulary and connect it to new information.

Write (How did the variety of people and faiths impact ancient Indian culture?)
A great way to get your student thinking about this is by connecting it to the global society we have today. Almost all areas of the world have become "melting pots," and every new person or faith adds a layer to the local culture. Talk with your student about how your country's culture has been impacted by the introduction of new people and their beliefs, music, language, etc.

Review (Ancient Indian Governments and Empires)
Again, you should divide up this page. Have your student read a section and then stop and discuss what they learned. Then go back and highlight any vocabulary words for review. Another great thing to do in this section is write out the dates and important events on a whiteboard or paper so that they are visible when your student completes the timeline activity.

Learning Styles

Auditory learners may enjoy talking through the history of ancient India and telling stories that go along with each time period. This will make it personal for them and allow you to correct any mistakes or misconceptions.

Visual learners may enjoy drawing colorful notes and diagrams for each section of their reading. Adding different colors and images helps them to organize and retain information. Some good options are a map of ancient India with locations marked, the caste pyramid, the Buddhist wheel, etc.

Kinesthetic learners may enjoy acting out skits from each time period. They could pretend to be a member of the Indus River Valley civilization and act out what they do in their home. Then they could pretend to be Ashoka experiencing regret for his mistakes. This will bring the history alive for them and help them retain information.

Extension Activities

Vocabulary Hunt

Write all the vocabulary words on index cards with their definitions on the opposite side. Hide the cards and have your student hunt for them. When they find a card, they should tell you the definition. If they get it right, they get to keep it. If they get it wrong, they have to give it back and have you hide it again. Keep going until they find all the cards and get the definitions correct.

Mapping

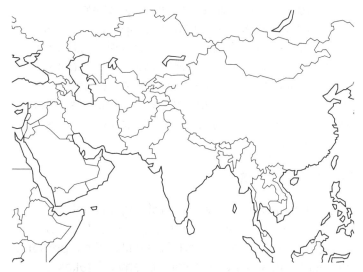

Print off a map like this one that only shows the political outlines and have your student use resources like maps, atlases, and their textbook to mark the locations of the following:

- Modern-day India, Pakistan, and Afghanistan
- The approximate location of the Indus River Valley
- The trade routes of the Indus River Valley civilization to Mesopotamia
- The assumed route of the Aryan civilization into India
- The approximate location where the Buddha lived
- The approximate size of the Magadha kingdom
- The approximate size of the Mauryan Empire during the rule of Ashoka the Great
- The location of the Kalinga kingdom

Answer Key

Write *(How did the variety of people and faiths impact ancient Indian culture?)*

Answers will vary. Possible answers: The migration of the Aryan people to ancient India brought new language and religion, which have impacted the social structure of India to this day. When many people from different backgrounds live together, they start to share their ideas, beliefs, language, and values with each other. This can blend into a completely new culture that is unique to that area.

Write *(The Nanda dynasty had a great army and built a powerful kingdom, but their reign only lasted about 24 years. Why do you think that was?)*

Answers will vary. Possible answers: The Nanda rulers were extremely unpopular with the people of ancient India. There are stories that they came from a Shudra clan and killed the rightful rulers so that they could take over. They also taxed the people into poverty to pay for their large army and constant battles.

Practice *(Faith and Language Comparison)*

Answers will vary. Possible answers:

Hinduism	Both	Buddhism
based on the Vedas uses the caste system polytheistic salvation through rituals, good works, and meditation	believe in the concepts of samsara, karma, and moksha main goal is salvation or enlightenment (moksha)	focuses on individual improvement and does not worship any particular god believers spend time meditating on the Four Noble Truths and the Eightfold Path salvation through the release of all desire to achieve nirvana

Both Hinduism and Buddhism believe in a cycle of death and rebirth. Buddhists believe that the only way to achieve moksha is to let go of all earthly desires, and Hindus believe that one must perform the dharma properly and go through the cycles of rebirth and climb the castes until they are finally able to released by the cycle and rejoin Brahman.

Sanskrit	Both	English
52 letters ancient language holy language Indo-Iranian origin mostly unchanged different letter for each sound	phonetic Indo-European language	26 letters young language used worldwide Germanic origin constantly changing letters make different sounds depending on use

Sanskrit and English both originated in the Indo-European language family. Sanskrit is an ancient language that inspired the creation of other languages (like Hindi), and English was developed over several years from the Germanic branch. English is a regularly evolving language while Sanskrit has stayed the same for centuries.

Practice *(Ancient Indian Timeline)*

The timeline should include these items:

- A bar for the Indus River Valley civilization stretching from 3300–1700 BC
- A bar for the Vedic Period from 1750–500 BC
- A bar for the Magadha kingdom from 544–321 BC
- A bar for the Mauryan kingdom from 321–185 BC
- A point for the merging of the Mahajanapadas at 544 BC
- A point for the start of the Nanda dynasty at 345 BC
- A point for when Chandragupta replaces Dhana Nanda at 321 BC
- A point for when Ashoka became the ruler of the Mauryan Empire at about 273 BC
- A point for the defeat of Kalinga at about 261 BC

Quick Review

Refer to the statement your student circled in the Show What You Know section to self-assess their knowledge of the chapter concepts. Then to assist in determining if your student is ready to take the assessment, consider:

• Having your student explain how the locations of ancient India relate to those of modern-day Asia. For example, they should understand that the Indus River Valley civilization mostly lived in modern-day Pakistan and not India.

• Having your student discuss the sequence of events. It is not as important that they remember specific dates but that they understand the order that the various civilizations and events occurred.

• Having your student review the Hindu castes and what they meant for ancient Indians.

Chapter Assessment

Circle the correct answer(s) for each question.

1. The Indus River Valley is in which modern-day country?
   A. Afghanistan
   B. India
   C. China
   D. Pakistan

2. Who were the Aryan people before coming to India?
   A. farmers
   B. nomads
   C. sailors
   D. conquerors

3. The people of the Indus River Valley enjoyed which technology in their homes? Circle all correct answers.
   A. indoor toilets
   B. computers
   C. air-conditioning
   D. security cameras

4. What kind of job did the members of the Brahmin caste have?
   A. kings
   B. priests
   C. servants
   D. merchants

5. What language did the Aryan people originally speak?
   A. Vedic Sanskrit
   B. Classic Sanskrit
   C. Hindi
   D. English

6. Before becoming the Buddha, Siddartha Gautama was a(n) _____.
   A. butcher
   B. prince
   C. untouchable
   D. priest

7. If a faith is monotheistic, the people who practice it worship _____.
   A. many gods
   B. money
   C. one god
   D. a person

8. Sanskrit and English are both derived from the Indo-European language family, but they sound different because English came from the Germanic branch and Sanskrit came from the _____ branch.
   A. Indo-Iranian
   B. Italic
   C. Greek
   D. Anatolian

9. Which person wrote *The Ashtadhyayi*, a book with 3,959 rules that standardized the Sanskrit language?
   A. Chanakya
   B. Ashoka
   C. Dhana Nanda
   D. Panini

10. Which of the Mahajanapadas emerged as the largest kingdom in ca. 544 BC?
    A. Mauryan Empire
    B. Kalinga
    C. Magadha
    D. Avanti

11. Number these events so that they are in chronological order.

   A. _____ The Mahajanapadas are formed.

   B. _____ The caste system begins in ancient India.

   C. _____ Chanakya and Chandragupta team up to establish the Mauryan Empire.

   D. _____ The Harappans abandon their cities.

   E. _____ Ashoka defeats the kingdom of Kalinga.

   F. _____ The Harappans develop a strong trade economy.

   G. _____ The Nanda dynasty comes to power.

Read each sentence. Circle True or False.

12. True or False   Homes in the Harappan civilization had indoor plumbing.

13. True or False   Members of the Dalit caste worked as merchants and farmers.

14. True or False   Members of the Kshatriya caste were warriors and leaders.

15. True or False   Hinduism is a polytheistic religion.

16. True or False   Chandragupta Maurya was the last great leader of the Mauryan Empire.

Answer the following questions with complete sentences.

17. What was the dominant religion during the Vedic Period?

   ....

   ....

18. Why did the Nanda dynasty end?

   ....

   ....

19. Describe a typical home of the Harappan civilization.

   ....

   ....

20. Why were the people of lower castes drawn to Buddhism?

   ....

   ....

21. How is Buddhism different from Christianity?

   ....

   ....

Chapter Assessment Answer Key

1. D
2. B
3. A, C
4. B
5. A
6. B
7. C
8. A
9. D
10. C
11. A: 4, B: 3, C: 6, D: 2, E: 7, F: 1, G: 5
12. True
13. False
14. True
15. True
16. False
17. Answers may vary. Possible answer: The dominant religion during the Vedic Period was Hinduism.
18. Answers may vary. Possible answer: The Nanda dynasty ended because Dhana Nanda was a very unpopular ruler who overtaxed his people.
19. Answers may vary. Possible answer: The Harappan homes were built around a central courtyard in neighborhoods off of the main roads. They had indoor toilets, a well for fresh water, and flat roofs for extra space to work and rest.
20. Answers may vary. Possible answer: People of the lower castes were drawn to Buddhism because it did not maintain the caste system. Buddhists believe that anyone can achieve enlightenment, not just those of the Brahmin caste like Hindus.
21. Answers may vary. Possible answer: Buddhists do not believe in any gods, while Christians believe in God. Buddhists follow the teachings of the Buddha, while Christians follow the teachings of Jesus Christ. Buddhists believe that salvation comes through self-discipline and personal improvement, while Christians believe that salvation comes from God's grace and Christ's sacrifice.

Alternative Assessment

Project: Ancient Indian Historical Fiction

Project Requirements and Steps:

Write a short piece of historical fiction based on ancient India. You can choose to write a story about a character who lived in the Indus River Valley civilization, the Magadha kingdom, or the Mauryan Empire.

To write your story:

1. Create a character who lived during one of the above time periods.
2. Give them a name and answer the following questions:
   - How old are they?
   - What kind of family do they have, and what are some family members' names?
   - What is their religion?
   - What is their job or their family's job?
   - Where do they live?

3. Decide which historical event will impact your character's life.
4. Decide which important ancient Indian people they will interact with.
5. Come up with a problem and a solution to that problem that is historically accurate.

Make sure your story has the following :

- A title related to the chapter
- Reference to the time period you chose to write on
- Plot progression or a clear storyline
- Well-developed characters
- Literary elements such as figurative language
- Connection to the chapter through setting, characters, plot, etc.

Take a moment to plan out your story and review the rubric before starting your project.

Alternative Assessment Rubric

Use the following rubric to grade your student's assessment.

	4	3	2	1	Points
Accuracy and Relevance	The work has many characteristics or examples that tie it to an historical event or time period. The connections to history are academically advanced and indicate a great deal of effort.	The work has several characteristics or examples that tie it to an historical event or time period.	The work has one or two characteristics or examples that tie it to an historical event or time period.	The work has no connections to history.	
Quality	The work exceeds expectations. The storyline is very interesting and high quality.	The work is of good quality, but there is some room for improvement.	The work has many areas that could be improved.	The work is very low quality.	
Creativity	The work is creative and original and very interesting to the reader.	The work is somewhat creative and original and interesting to the reader.	The work is not very creative or original, but it is interesting to the reader.	The work is not creative or interesting.	
Grammar and Mechanics	The work has no grammar or punctuation issues and uses advanced vocabulary.	The work contains a few grammar or punctuation mistakes and uses age-appropriate vocabulary.	The work contains several grammar and punctuation mistakes and uses age-appropriate vocabulary.	The work contains a distracting number of grammar and punctuation mistakes and uses overly-simplified vocabulary.	

Total Points _____/16

Average _____

Discover! SOCIAL STUDIES • GRADE 6 • CHAPTER 5 ASSESSMENT

101

Lesson Objectives

By the end of this lesson, your student will be able to:

- locate the sites of the Shang and Zhou ancient Chinese civilizations on a map
- describe the geographic features of China
- describe the importance of the Huang He River

Supporting Your Student

Read (Mountains and Plains)

It may be helpful to have a physical map of China available as your student reads about its prominent mountains and grasslands and their locations. For example, as your student reads about Mount Everest and how it is part of the Himalayan mountain range, have your student point out its location on the map. Ask your student to assess the whereabouts of the mountains in China. For example, "The Himalayas span across a region between southern China and northern India." By pointing out the geographic features in China, it gives your student a frame of reference and helps them gauge the distances between them.

Write (How do the geographic features of western China differ from eastern China?)

Help your student to locate these geographic features by first encouraging them to point them out on the provided map. Encourage your student to start from western China and work their way toward eastern China. Once your student locates and circles all the geographic features, discuss how the west compares with the east. Your student may notice that the west is colored in brown or tan to represent mountains and the east is colored in green to represent river valleys.

Read (Rivers, Gorges, and Canyons)

As your student reads this section, it may be helpful to retrieve online images of these geographic features so your student can better understand the differences between gorges and canyons and why the Huang He (Yellow) River is yellow. To help your student visualize these features on a map, pull out a physical map of China and have your student locate these geographic features. Encourage your student to think about how

geographic features influenced the development of the Shang and Zhou civilizations.

Learning Styles

Auditory learners may enjoy listening to a podcast on the geographic features or ancient civilization in China.

Visual learners may enjoy watching a nature show on the unique geographic features in China or a documentary on how ancient civilizations developed philosophy and poetry from the geographic features of China.

Kinesthetic learners may enjoy making a three-dimensional map of China to highlight its geographic features, using any arts and crafts supplies.

Extension Activities

Make a Pop-Up Book

With your student, make a three-dimensional pop-up book of the important geographical features of China, such as mountains, rivers, deserts, and plains. Encourage your student to keep it simple and choose up to five geographic features to showcase in the book. For each geographic feature, list a few facts including its location, size, and importance. Your student may reference the worktext or do research online.

Compare and Contrast Ancient Civilizations

With your student, compare and contrast the ancient civilizations Shang and Zhou. Investigate how and when these two civilizations flourished, notable achievements in art and philosophy, and how the geographic features around them influenced their famous works in poetry. Showcase your student's findings by creating an online presentation or poster board.

Features and Resources of Ancient China

Answer Key

Write *(How do the geographic features of western China differ from eastern China?)*
Assist your student to make sure that Mount Everest, K2, the Yellow Mountains, and the grasslands of Dzungaria and Manchuria are properly circled on the map. Answers may vary. Possible answers: The geographic features of western China differ from eastern Asia in that it is drier and mountainous compared to a wetter eastern Asia; western China has more mountains and grasslands compared to more rivers and river valleys in eastern Asia.

Practice

1. Gobi Desert
2. Yangtze River
3. river valley
4. Huang He (Yellow) River
5. Mount Everest
6. grasslands or steppes

Show What You Know

1. E
2. The area circled is the general area where the Shang and Zhou civilizations settled in ancient China.
3. Answers may vary. Possible answers: The Himalayas are located in south China/north Nepal. The vGobi Desert is located in the northern Himalayas/southern Mongolia. Grasslands (steppes) are Dzungaria in northwestern China or Manchuria in northeastern China.
4. True

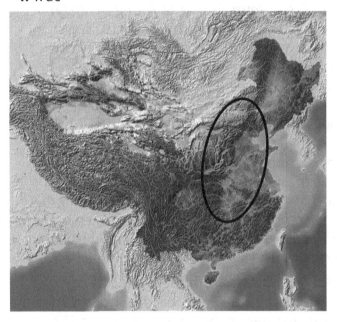

Lesson Objectives

By the end of this lesson, your student will be able to:

- explain why the Chinese called their land the Middle Kingdom
- identify key events in the development of the Shang and Zhou dynasties
- explain how the Mandate of Heaven was used to justify the Zhou leaders' rebellion against the Shang

Supporting Your Student

Read (*Key Events From the Shang Dynasty*)
To help your student visualize the social class of the Shang dynasty, have your student write down the members and their specific roles in society by creating a pyramid. Guide your student to divide the pyramid into different parts based on the groups of people with the same status (hierarchy). For example, because there were four groups of people in the Shang dynasty, your student should divide the pyramid into four parts. Encourage your student to complete the pyramid by explaining that the top represents the most important members of the kingdom (kings and aristocrats) and the bottom represents the least important citizens (peasants).

Read (*Key Events From the Zhou Dynasty*)
To help your student better understand Confucianism, have them research the life of Confucius and his beliefs about society. Encourage your student to investigate Confucius's famous book, *The Analects*, which details his famous philosophies.

Practice
Help your student fill in the bubbles by referring back to the worktext and writing down important points from each section. As your student completes the bubbles, encourage them to think about how each key event influenced the way people thought and behaved, inspiring the creation of the Mandate of Heaven, decentralized government, and Confucianism.

Learning Styles

Auditory learners may enjoy listening to a song in Chinese or an audio file on how to pronounce basic Chinese words.

Visual learners may enjoy watching a documentary on the rise and fall of ancient Chinese civilizations, their famous philosophies, religion, and art.

Kinesthetic learners may enjoy making models or figurines of members of the Shang dynasty social classes, such as kings and aristocrats, military, merchants, and peasants.

Extension Activities

Learn Simplified Chinese Characters!
Simplified Chinese characters are commonly used in mainland China and Singapore. With your student, use an online search engine to learn how to write basic words such as *love*, *horse*, *rain*, and *wind* using Simplified Chinese characters. Encourage your student to exercise patience and practice brush strokes as needed.

Make a Timeline
With your student, make a timeline of the major events that occurred in the Shang and Zhou dynasties including wars, invention of art, science and technology, creation of philosophy, and poetry. Encourage your student to get creative and design the timeline as a three-dimensional model, a flip-book, or a video. This activity will help your student extrapolate and filter the importance of the information that they find and organize them in a clear and succinct fashion.

Answer Key

Write *(Describe the social class and the concept of divination in the Shang dynasty.)*

Answers may vary. Possible answers: The social class was made up of four classes: the aristocracy, the military, artisans and craftsmen, and peasants. The king and aristocracy governed the kingdom. The military fought on foot; artisans and craftsmen worked with bronze; peasants worked as farmers.

Write *(What was the Mandate of Heaven and how did it end the Shang dynasty?)*

Answers may vary. Possible answers: The Mandate of Heaven determines whether a king (or any ordinary citizen) is fit to rule based on heaven's approval. The Zhou leaders saw that the Shang king was unfit to rule and used the Mandate to justify the Zhou leaders' rebellion against the king.

Write *(What are some principles of Confucianism?)*

Answers may vary. Possible answer: Confucianism is a philosophy created by Confucius, a famous Chinese philosopher. He believed in tradition and that every person should strive to be respectful and fit into his or her place in society.

Practice

Answers may vary. Possible answers:

- Key events from the Shang dynasty: the development of a social class and divination
- Key events from the Zhou dynasty: the development of a decentralized government and philosophy (Confucianism)
- Mandate of Heaven: four-rule philosophy about whether a king (or any ordinary citizen) is fit to rule based on heaven's approval

Show What You Know

1. Answers may vary. Possible answers: The Chinese believed that they were in the middle of the world, surrounded by natural barriers that kept the barbarians out.
2. A
3. D
4. C
5. False

Art, Education, and Philosophy in Ancient China

Lesson Objectives

By the end of this lesson, your student will be able to:

- identify the kinds of classical art produced during the Zhou dynasty
- describe the importance of education during the Zhou dynasty
- identify Confucius as a philosopher who greatly influenced China

Supporting Your Student

Read (Bronze, Jade, and Lacquer)

As your student reads this section, it may be helpful to pull up additional images of Chinese bronze, jade, and lacquer art so your student can better visualize these objects. To help your student understand the importance of these classical art pieces, encourage them to look into their uses and net worth in modern times. For example, where are dings (Chinese bronze vessels) used in China today? How much was a ding worth in ancient times? How much would one cost today?

Read (Education)

As your student reads this section, it may be helpful for your student to read or watch video clips on the education system of ancient China using an online search engine. As your student reads or watches, encourage them to compare and contrast the education system in ancient China to the education system that they are familiar with today. For example, the education system of the Zhou dynasty was separated into two schools: state (for nobility) and village (for ordinary citizens). State and village schools are equivalent to modern-day private and public schools, respectively. However, while there are all-boys and all-girls schools today, only boys were allowed to attend school to receive an education. Girls had to stay home to learn childcare, cooking, and cleaning from their mothers.

Practice

Encourage your student to reread the worktext to fill in the bubble diagram. Ask your student to identify at least two features for each bubble directly from the

readings, additional research, or own life experiences. For example, Confucianism had several influences in ancient and modern society such as the development of schools, the creation of a civil service examination, and an increase in government jobs.

Learning Styles

Auditory learners may enjoy listening to a podcast on the life, teachings, and philosophies of Confucius.

Visual learners may enjoy watching a documentary on the Bronze Age of ancient China or how valuable materials such as jade and lacquer were used in the Zhou dynasty and beyond.

Kinesthetic learners may enjoy learning a traditional Chinese dance that implements ancient Chinese instruments such as the bell (bo).

Extension Activities

Create Art Videos

With your student, create an art video or a series of short art videos that introduce popular classical art in the Zhou dynasty, including valuable items made from bronze, jade, and lacquer. Encourage your student to be creative with their art video, such as adding animation, sound, or captions, and describe each art piece using interactive pictures or videos.

Create Ancient Chinese Lacquerware

With your student, create ancient Chinese lacquerware by obtaining plain white or gray plastic bowls or cups. Using paint as an alternative to lacquer, have your student paint each bowl or cup depicting popular Chinese images of nature, such as mountains, rivers, and birds, or simple Chinese calligraphy. You may wish to assist your student with painting images of nature by looking through photos of ancient Chinese lacquerware or pulling up photos of the Huang He and Yangtze River valleys.

Answer Key

Explore

Answers may vary. Possible answers: All items are made of bronze. Some items have symmetrical lines, while others are asymmetrical. Some items feature animals such as dragons, while others feature nature. Some items are tall and deep, while others are short and flat.

Write *(How was bronze, jade, and lacquer used in the Zhou dynasty? Why were they important?)*

Answers may vary. Possible answers: Bronze was used to make vessels for ceremonies and rituals. Jade was worn by royalty as pendants and bracelets. Lacquer was used to color bowls and cups. Bronze and jade were important because they symbolized power and status. Lacquer was important as art to depict nature.

Write *(Why was education important in the Zhou dynasty?)*

Answers may vary. Possible answers: It was tradition for kings to select well-educated individuals to assist them in managing their kingdoms. Boys were expected to receive an education so they could fulfill jobs in the government as adults.

Write *(How did Confucianism influence China?)*

Answers may vary. Possible answers: Confucius was a famous philosopher and teacher who believed that people should be respectful and fair in order to create a harmonious society. His beliefs, known as Confucianism, and his teachings are written in a book called The Analects, which have been used in education throughout Chinese history and helped create ancient Chinese laws.

Practice

Answers may vary. Possible answers:

- Examples of Classical Art: vessels like ding, fangding, gui, and zun; jade bracelets, pendants, and rings; lacquerware including cups, bowls, furniture, and screenss

- Importance of Education: to fulfill government jobs as adults, to learn and engage in Confucian principles

- Influence of Confucianism: creation of ancient Chinese laws, development of schools and emphasis on receiving an education (boys), creation of more jobs in the government (boys), development of *The Analects*, development of the civil service examination to recruit talented people to fulfill positions in the government (boys)

Show What You Know

1. Answers may vary. Possible answers: ding, fangding, gui, and zun
2. A, D
3. lacquerware
4. C
5. D

LESSON 34
Comparing Philosophies of Ancient China

Lesson Objectives

By the end of this lesson, your student will be able to:

- describe the principles of Taoism
- describe Legalism as a philosophy
- compare and contrast Taoism, Legalism, and Confucianism

Supporting Your Student

Read (Taoism)

As your student reads this section, it may be helpful for them to watch introductory video clips so they can better understand the origins and principles of Taoism. You may choose to help your student relate Taoist principles to their own lives, such as the importance of simplicity, patience, and compassion. For example, ask your student to identify a simple feature or aspect in life, such as water. Then ask your student why or how it (water) affects their own life and the people in society. Do the same for patience and compassion. As your student relates these ideas to themselves, they can develop a fundamental understanding and appreciate the relatability of Taoist principles to modern-day society.

Read (Legalism)

As your student reads this section, it may be helpful for your student to use an online search engine to investigate the Warring States period of the Zhou dynasty or read and watch video clips on the origins of the Qin dynasty. These resources can help your student better grasp the prolonged period of unrest during the fall of the Zhou dynasty and how these conditions led to the development of legalist principles.

Practice

Your student may struggle to compare and contrast ancient Chinese philosophies. Encourage your student to re-read Taoism, Legalism, and Confucianism from the worktext, or use an online search engine to dive deeper into the material. Then ask your student to highlight, circle, or jot down similarities and differences of these philosophies. If your student still has trouble finding similarities among all three philosophies, ask your student to look at them holistically and identify common key words. For example, although Taoism, Legalism, and Confucianism are very different, they were all created with the goals of improving human nature, society, and preventing or ending conflicts.

Learning Styles

Auditory learners may enjoy listening to a podcast or recording on ancient Chinese philosophies, including Taoism, Legalism, and Confucianism and how they influenced society.

Visual learners may enjoy reading excerpts or adaptations of *The Analects* (the book of Confucius philosophies and teachings) or the *Tao Te Ching* (the book of Lao Tzu's philosophies).

Kinesthetic learners may enjoy putting together a minidocumentary on famous Chinese philosophers and their philosophies.

Extension Activities

Ancient Chinese Philosophies

With your student, reenact ancient Chinese philosophies such as Taoism, Legalism, or Confucianism by writing a short script and putting on a play. This activity may require a few people to play different characters from ancient China. For example, if your student is interested in putting on a play about Confucianism, characters that need to be played may include Confucius and his students. As your student writes a script, encourage them to focus on specific principles of Confucianism and how they influenced ancient China. Examples may include the development of schools for boys to learn Confucian principles and partake in government duties as adults or how Confucian principles of duty and service to society led to the creation of the civil service exam.

What Would They Say or Do?

Have your student write down three to four scenarios that yield positive or negative outcomes and predict what ancient Chinese philosophers would say or do.

Comparing Philosophies of Ancient China

Scenario 1: People stole food from a market because they were hungry.

- What would Lao Tzu say or do?
- What would Han Feizi say or do?
- What would Confucius say or do?

Scenario 2: A person donates money to aid in the rescue of sea turtles.

- What would Lao Tzu say or do?
- What would Han Feizi say or do?
- What would Confucius say or do?

Scenario 3: A classmate gets picked on by another student.

- What would Lao Tzu say or do?
- What would Han Feizi say or do?
- What would Confucius say or do?

Encourage your student to have fun, but have them be specific and provide reasons to justify their answers. Have your student write down their answers by creating a book or video clip.

Answer Key

Explore

Answers may vary. Possible answers: The drawing indicates that trying requires failing and failing requires trying. When you try and fail several times, trying can lead to success. "The product of trying and failing is success." This is a philosophy because it is a basic idea that influences behavior and encourages people to persevere.

Write *(What are the principles of Taoism?)*

Answers may vary. Possible answers: simplicity, patience, and compassion; going with the flow; letting go; harmony

Write *(What are the principles of Legalism?)*

Answers may vary. Possible answers: People will not sacrifice for each other unless forced to. People will most likely kill another if it favors them. Strict laws must be created to direct people's behavior for the good of society.

Write *(What are the main ideas of Taoism, Legalism, and Confucianism?)*

Answers may vary. Possible answers: Taoism says people should give up worldly desires in favor of nature and the Tao. Legalism says society needs a system of strict laws and harsh punishments to control human behavior. Confucianism says people should put the needs of their families and communities first.

Show What You Know

1. Answers may vary. Possible answers: simplicity, patience, and compassion; going with the flow; letting go; harmony
2. C
3. B
4. A, C, E

Achievements of the Qin Dynasty

Lesson Objectives

By the end of this lesson, your student will be able to:

- describe the achievements of the Qin dynasty
- describe the purpose for the construction of the Great Wall

Supporting Your Student

Explore

Guide your student to answer this question by looking at the images in Explore. Encourage them to use examples from daily life or previous reading to better understand purpose and achievement. For example, what is the function or purpose of sculptures? From previous reading, your student may know that ancient civilizations created sculptures to represent important features such as religion in their society. Your student may surmise that the image of the Terra-Cotta Army soldiers represent law, order, or protection. Your student may hypothesize that they were major achievements because they were plentiful and crafted in detail.

Read *(Standardized Written Language)*

As your student reads this section, it may be helpful for them to have a frame of reference of the written languages that existed (and still exist) in Chinese history. Your student may do this by using an online search engine to investigate how written language in China evolved over time. For example, from the Oracle script (Shang dynasty), Bronze script (Zhou dynasty), and Small-seal script (Qin dynasty) of ancient times to Simplified and Traditional characters used in modern-day Chinese culture. Encourage your student to think about the pros and cons of having a unified (standardized) and decentralized (nonstandardized) written language. This will help your student better understand how standardized written language was an achievement in the Qin dynasty.

Practice

Help your student complete this table by referring back to the worktext as necessary. Encourage your student to be detailed when describing the

importance of each achievement. For example, the invention of the iron crossbows were important because they were faster, delivered more power, and were more accurate than traditional composite bows. Reinforce concepts by asking your student to draw an image that can be associated with each achievement. For example, to emphasize the power and strength of crossbows, your student may draw a crossbow with a lightning bolt.

Learning Styles

Auditory learners may enjoy learning basic Chinese words, phrases, or songs.

Visual learners may enjoy watching a show or documentary on the achievements from the Qin dynasty such as the Great Wall, the Lingqu Canal, the Terra-Cotta Army, and iron weapons.

Kinesthetic learners may enjoy reconstructing the Great Wall of China from arts and crafts supplies such as legos, cardboard boxes, sticks, rulers, glue, rocks, and/or any common household items.

Extension Activities

Learn to Write in Small-Seal Script

Have your student learn how to write basic words in Small-seal script by using an online search engine to look up images. Encourage your student to compare the Small-seal script to other variations of written language in ancient China such as Bronze script and Oracle script. Have your student compare them with modern-day characters such as Simplified or Traditional. Ask how written language has evolved throughout Chinese history.

Create Your Own Terra-Cotta Army Soldiers

With your student, create your own Terra-Cotta Army soldiers by using modeling clay. As your student sculpts these soldiers, encourage them to pay attention to the designs of the original soldiers, such as the weapons, armor, chariots, and helmets they may have worn or carried.

Answer Key

Explore

Answers may vary. Possible answers: the Great Wall to keep barbarians or invaders out, to unify China, the Lingqu Canal to connect the Li and Xiang Rivers, to transport goods from one region to another, to control floods and water supply, the Terra-Cotta Army soldiers to represent power and authority, to represent the need to guard or prevent invaders from the north

Write *(What was the importance of a standardized written language?)*

Answers may vary. Possible answers: to unify China, to make written language and communication simpler for people who could read and write

Write *(What was the Terra-Cotta Army and why was it important?)*

Answers may vary. Possible answers: The Terra-Cotta Army soldiers were life-size sculptures buried with the king after his death. They were important because they were meant to guard him in the afterlife.

Write *(What was the purpose of the construction of the Great Wall?)*

Answers may vary. Possible answer: The Great Wall was built to keep northern invaders out.

Practice

Answers may vary. Possible answers:

Achievements of the Qin Dynasty	Why They Were Important	Draw an Example of Each Achievement
Unified Written Language	This helped to unify the country.	Drawings will vary.
The Iron Industry	This helped to create strong weapons that were more accurate.	Drawings will vary.
The Great Wall	This helped to keep northern invaders out.	Drawings will vary.

Show What You Know

1. Answers may vary. Possible answers: Standardized written language helped people to better communicate and engage in trade and warfare. It also unified China and influenced the small-seal script as seen in modern-day Chinese written languages.

2. A, B, E

3. B

4. Answers may vary. Possible answers: Legalism, because the Great Wall of China was built as a single border wall by several people the king saw as disloyal and unjust to the system of strict laws. As punishment, he enslaved people to build the Great Wall of China. Strength, because despite the cruel and hard labor that these workers endured, they were resilient and many of them sacrificed their lives to protect China. Unity, because the Great Wall of China was created with a common goal shared by all its people, which was to protect China from northern invaders. This common goal united China.

Civil Service and Currency in China

Lesson Objectives

By the end of this lesson, your student will be able to:

- identify the purpose of the civil service exam in the Han government
- trace the use of currency in China

Supporting Your Student

Read (The Civil Service Exam)

As your student reads through this section in the worktext, it may be helpful to find online videos that describe the origins, purpose, and relevance of the civil service exam during the Han dynasty. Encourage your student to think about the influences of the civil service exam in ancient China and their lasting effects in present-day China and beyond. To help pique your student's interest, have them think about exams that they have taken and potential exams they may take for higher education.

Read (Currency)

Help your student visualize currency used in ancient China by using an online search engine to search for additional images. For example, as your student reads about the benefits of using cowrie shells as money, have them look at the corresponding image and evaluate their sizes, shapes, marks, and weights. Encourage your student to do the same for different types of currency, including metal coins, paper bills, and banknotes. Then discuss with your student the evolution of Chinese currency from ancient to modern times.

Practice

Assist your student in completing the bubble map by asking them to refer back to the worktext. As your student re-reads the main topics of this lesson, encourage them to write down or highlight important points in each section. For example, as your student reads about the civil service exam, ask your student the purpose and relevance of the exam in the Han dynasty and in succeeding Chinese dynasties. Your student may respond by stating that the civil service exam was developed to select well-educated and talented individuals to fulfill positions in the government. Your student may also explain that the exam influenced the gaokao, the modern-day version of the civil service exam that is used in China to recruit top students into reputable schools. These examples are major features of the civil service exam.

Learning Styles

Auditory learners may enjoy listening to an audio file about how the civil service exam was created in the Han dynasty.

Visual learners may enjoy watching a video about the construction, purpose, and significance of the Great Wall of China.

Kinesthetic learners may enjoy constructing a model of the Great Wall of China using materials such as modeling clay, cardboard, or any other arts and crafts supplies.

Extension Activities

Chinese Currency Timeline

With your student, create a timeline that shows the evolution of Chinese currency from ancient to modern times. Encourage your student to study the differences in composition, size, shape, color, and texture of ancient and modern Chinese currencies by using an online search engine. As your student studies these differences, discuss how Chinese currency improved over time. Showcase your student's research by having them create a booklet, poster, or online presentation.

Create a Modern Civil Service Exam

With your student, create a modern civil service exam featuring some of the topics that were used in the civil service exam of ancient China, such as Confucianism, mathematics, military, geography, and poetry. Your student may wish to incorporate any other topics of interest, including science or philosophy. Then ask your student to imagine themselves as a hiring manager of a reputable government organization. Encourage your student to think about the possible questions they might ask potential employees to answer. As your student brainstorms, discuss how their list of questions could be used to determine how qualified a candidate is and to assess the skills and talents necessary for employees to succeed in the organization.

Answer Key

Write *(What was the purpose of the civil service exam in the Han government?)*

Answers may vary. Possible answers: Emperor Gaozu, the first emperor of the Han dynasty, was not able to run the entire empire by himself due to its large size. Therefore, he decided to create a system that could select highly educated ministers to help run the empire.

Write *(What kind of currency was used during the Qin dynasty?)*

Answers may vary. Possible answers: Bronze coins that had the same shape, size, weight, and mark, to represent a specific value.

Practice

Answers may vary. Possible answers:

- Features of the Civil Service Exam: It was established during the Han dynasty in 207 BC by the first Han Emperor, Gaozu. The exam was created to select highly educated ministers to help run the empire. Many of the questions that were asked on the civil service exam covered Confucianism, mathematics, geography, military, calligraphy, and writing poetry. The civil service exam was based on merit and not on a person's family status.

- Features of Currency: Emperor Shi Huangdi standardized currency in the Qin dynasty that allowed metal coins of the same value to have the same features, including size, weight, shape, and mark. Cowrie shells were the earliest form of currency in ancient China. They were useful because they were small and easy to carry around. The renminbi is the currency used in China today and features metal coins and banknotes.

Show What You Know

1. A, D, E
2. Answers may vary. Possible answers: Shell money was the earliest form of currency in ancient China. These shells were small, easy to carry around, and were found in the seas that surrounded the country.
3. A

Lesson Objectives

By the end of this lesson, your student will be able to:

- describe the social changes during the Han dynasty
- identify the problems and benefits of the Silk Road
- contrast Mahayana Buddhism with another religion

Supporting Your Student

Read *(Problems and Benefits of the Silk Road)*

As your student reads this section in the worktext, it may be helpful to retrieve an image or map that shows the Silk Road trade routes by using an online search engine. Ask your student to identify the countries and geographic features that the trade routes cross. For example, when your student reads about the problems of the Silk Road, such as sandstorms and rugged landforms, have them point out the names and locations of deserts and mountains. Encourage your student to dive deeper into the lesson by watching videos on the Silk Road. This will help your student better understand the influences the Silk Road had in ancient times and their lasting effects in modern-day society.

Read *(Mahayana Buddhism and Hinduism)*

Help your student better understand the unique features of Mahayana Buddhism and Hinduism by using an online search engine to retrieve images or videos on these two major religions. For example, as your student reads about nirvana, discuss with them the teachings and accomplishments of Siddartha Guatama and how they influenced the culture of ancient Chinese civilizations like the Han dynasty. Encourage your student to research the origins and features of Hinduism and why some of their principles are similar to Mahayana Buddhism.

Learning Styles

Auditory learners may enjoy creating a podcast on the Silk Road and discuss its origins, importance, benefits, problems, and contributions to the world today.

Visual learners may enjoy creating an infographic on the Silk Road and displaying it for family or friends. They may also enjoy watching a documentary on the influences of Mahayana Buddhism or Hinduism in ancient and modern times.

Kinesthetic learners may enjoy tracing the routes of the Silk Road on paper by creating a physical map.

Extension Activities

Silk Road Flashcards

Have your student create flash cards featuring products and ideas that were exchanged on the Silk Road, such as silk, gunpowder, fruits and vegetables, technology, religion, and philosophy. Your student may also wish to include the problems and benefits of the Silk Road. Ask your student to write the names of products or ideas on one side of the card and describe their unique characteristics on the other side of the card. For example, gunpowder was a valuable product that was heavily exchanged on the Silk Road. Some of gunpowder's unique characteristics include its creation by the Chinese during the Han dynasty and that it was primarily used in firearms.

Comic Strip

Ask your student to create a comic strip in which they illustrate the life of Siddhartha Guatama, the founder of Buddhism. This will serve as a brief visual biography and should display a good understanding of Buddha's life and accomplishments. Remind your student that they are being evaluated on ideas and effort, and not artistic talent.

Answer Key

Write *(What were some of the social changes in the Han dynasty?)*

Answers may vary. Possible answers: Elimination of severe corporal punishment and the establishment of a rigid social hierarchy.

Write *(Did the benefits of the Silk Road outweigh the problems? Why or why not?)*

Answers may vary. Possible answers: Yes, the benefits outweighed the problems—the Silk Road allowed people to trade important items such as silk, spices, fruits and vegetables, livestock, tools, religious objects, technology, and gunpowder. The Silk Road was also important for the spread of religions such as Mahayana Buddhism and Hinduism. Without the Silk Road, there would not be a need for more jobs in farming, iron work, and commerce. The expansion of economic ties with other parts of the world besides China may also not have occurred. No, the benefits did not outweigh the problems—bad weather, rugged cliffs, lack of safety and security, and theft were all problems that people encountered on the Silk Road. The Silk Road also led to the spread of infectious diseases, such as the bubonic plague, which killed one-third of Europe's population.

Write *(What are two similarities between Mahayana Buddhism and Hinduism?)*

Answers may vary. Possible answers: Samsara, the continuous cycle of birth, death, and rebirth, the emphasis of compassion towards people

Show What You Know

1. Answers may vary. Possible answers: The top class was made of the emperor, aristocrats, and government officials. People of the middle class were skilled laborers like farmers and iron workers. The bottom class was made of unskilled laborers like merchants, servants, and slaves.

2. B, E

3. A, B, D, E

4. D

5. A, D, E

6. A, B, C, D

Lesson Objectives

By the end of this lesson, your student will review the following big ideas from Chapter 6.

- China has many geographic features, including the Huang He River. (Lesson 31)
- The Shang and Zhou dynasties were located on the eastern side of China. Key developments in the Shang and Zhou dynasties included contributions and vessels made of jade and bronze. (Lesson 32)
- The Zhou dynasty created the Mandate of Heaven to justify the rebellions against the Shang dynasty. Education was important to the Zhou dynasty as they had state schools for the rich. (Lesson 33)
- Confucius was a philosopher who influenced China. Taoism, Legalism, and Confucianism were philosophies practiced in ancient China. (Lesson 34)
- The Qin dynasty was known for building the Great Wall of China. (Lesson 35)
- The Han dynasty created the civil service exam. The currencies in ancient China varied from cowrie shells to paper bills. (Lesson 36)
- The Han dynasty was known for the Silk Road and Mahayana Buddhism. (Lesson 37)

Supporting Your Student

Review (Philosophies)
You may want to further explain Mahayana Buddhism and Hinduism. Discuss with your student that Buddhism and Hinduism are still practiced today. Buddhism is China's main religion, though other religions are gaining more followers. Hinduism was actually founded in India. India is located near China. Most of the people in India practice Hinduism.

Write (Describe how the people during the Zhou dynasty lived. What was their education like? What did they create?)
For these questions, you may want to discuss the state schools and the subjects they learned in those schools. Discuss the bowls and vessels that they created. Also, discuss the materials that they used and why they used those materials to make those vessels.

Practice (Philosophies Venn Diagram)
With this Venn diagram, your student only has to choose four out of the seven sections. You may want to reread the review sections. Have your student take notes about each of the three philosophies, then compare and contrast them.

Learning Styles

Auditory learners may enjoy a documentary about ancient China. Your student may want to select a topic that interests them the most. It could be education, a certain dynasty, Taoism, Legalism, Confucius, or the geography of China.

Visual learners may enjoy looking at pictures of artifacts from ancient China. See if they can tell what those artifacts were made of. Your student will need to research artifacts first. They may want to choose one of the dynasties (Zhou, Shang, Qin, Han) and see images of these artifacts.

Kinesthetic learners may enjoy replicating an artifact from a photo or image found on the internet. Your student can use craft supplies to make this artifact. Have your student think about what material it may have been made from. Then your student will have an idea about what color to make the artifact.

Extension Activities

Silk Road Game
Play a Silk Road game with your student and others up to five total players. First, create a set of 20 cards including 4 gold cards, 4 spices cards, 4 silk cards, 4 gunpowder cards, and 4 crops cards. Shuffle the cards and deal them out. The object of the game is to acquire 4 of a kind. You do this by trading cards with the other members of the game. Your student may trade with the other member or choose not to. The first member of the game to acquire all 4 of the same kind of cards wins.

Check Out the Chinese Currency

Have your student look at current Chinese money. Have them compare it to their currency. Have them note the similarities and differences. You may also have your student look up former currencies from ancient China.

Answer Key

Write *(Describe how the people during the Zhou dynasty lived. What was their education like? What did they create?)*

Answers will vary, but it may include the following information:

The Zhou dynasty had state schools for royalty. They learned math, reading, philosophy, military, music, and writing. The people in the Zhou dynasty made vessels out of bronze and jade.

Write *(What is the Han dynasty's main contribution? What is the Qin dynasty's main contribution? Describe their benefits and drawbacks.)*

The Han dynasty's biggest contribution was the Silk Road. That is what they are mainly known for. The benefit of the Silk Road was the ability to get food and supplies. Drawbacks were the spread of disease and safety concerns. The Qin dynasty's main contribution was the Great Wall of China. The benefit of it is that it kept out invaders. The drawback was that many people died trying to build it.

Practice *(Vocabulary Blanks Activity)*

1. Zhou
2. exam
3. Confucius
4. bronze
5. state
6. artwork

Practice *(Philosophies Venn Diagram)*

Answers will vary. Possible answers:

1. A similarity between Taoism and Confucianism was their focus on being in harmony.

2. The difference in Legalism was its focus on negativity and showing humans as thinking only of themselves.

3. A similarity among all philosophies was that all of them provided requirements or laws to follow.

4. Taoism was different because it included animals or nature with humans.

Practice *(Ordering Vocabulary)*

1. cowrie shells: This was the earliest currency and was made out of shells.

2. paper bills: These were used as money and made out of paper.

3. renminbi: This is used today as currency.

Quick Review

Refer to the statement your student circled in the Show What You Know section to self-assess their knowledge of the chapter concepts. Then to assist in determining if your student is ready to take the assessment, consider:

- Having your student explain how each dynasty (Zhou, Shang, Qin, Han) made different contributions to society.
- Having your student name the three philosophies of Taoism, Legalism, and Confucianism and having them describe some of their many similarities and differences.
- Having your student explain that China's geographic features include many mountains, plains, rivers, and 11 deserts.

118

Discover! SOCIAL STUDIES • GRADE 6 • CHAPTER 6 ASSESSMENT

Chapter Assessment

Circle the correct answer.

1. True or False   The Zhou and Shang dynasties were located in the western area of China.

2. True or False   The Huang He River was associated with the Zhou and Shang dynasties.

3. True or False   There are mountains, plains, and deserts in China.

4. True or False   The civil service exam was given to skilled men who reported to the emperor during the Han dynasty.

5. True or False   Paper bills were used as the first type of currency in China.

6. True or False   Cowrie shells were made of bronze, copper, and iron.

7. True or False   The Great Wall of China was built to impress other civilizations.

8. True or False   The Han dynasty's citizens were grouped based on their jobs.

9. True or False   One of the main problems with the Silk Road was the lack of traders and merchants wanting to trade.

10. True or False   People eagerly traded diseases with others on the Silk Road.

11. True or False   Mahayana Buddhism focuses on nirvana and enlightenment.

12. Why did the Chinese call their land the Middle Kingdom?

   A. They contributed the most to society.

   B. They believed they were in the center of the world.

   C. They had many strong leaders in their dynasties.

   D. They fought and won many battles and wars.

13. Which of the following was NOT a development in the Shang dynasty?

   A. calendars

   B. artwork

   C. astronomy

   D. math

14. Which of the following was NOT a development in the Zhou dynasty?

   A. Mandate of Heaven

   B. decentralized government

   C. Confucianism

   D. technology

15. Which of the following is NOT a part of the Mandate of Heaven?

A. There can only be one king at a time.

B. If people rebel, they should be saved by taking over the land.

C. A king has a right to rule according to Heaven.

D. A dynasty cannot rule forever.

Fill in the blank with the correct word.

16. The Zhou dynasty used _____ , which was a mixture of copper, tin, and lead, to make vessels.

17. The Zhou dynasty used a green stone called _____ to make ornaments.

18. _____ was a philosopher who wrote *The Analects*.

19. The students may have taken the _____ , which was a higher education exam.

20. At the _____ schools, royalty would learn reading, writing, military, math, music, and philosophy.

21. What are the four principles of Taoism?

....

....

22. Describe Legalism in a sentence.

....

....

23. Describe Confucianism in a sentence.

....

....

120

Discover! SOCIAL STUDIES • GRADE 6 • CHAPTER 6 ASSESSMENT

Chapter Assessment Answer Key

1. False
2. True
3. True
4. True
5. False
6. True
7. False
8. True
9. False
10. False
11. True
12. B
13. A
14. D
15. B
16. bronze
17. jade
18. Confucius
19. gaokao
20. state
21. simplicity, patience or compassion, going with the flow, letting go, and harmony
22. Legalism believes that people will do wrong instead of doing right.
23. Confucianism focuses on harmony and patience.

Discover! SOCIAL STUDIES • GRADE 6 • CHAPTER 6 ASSESSMENT

121

Alternative Assessment

Project: Create a Podcast

Project Requirements or Steps:

Create and present a podcast about ancient China. It should include information about the four dynasties, three philosophies, Buddhism religion, and common geographic features. Present your podcast to your friends and your instructor or just your instructor.

1. Brainstorm all of the parts of your podcast:

   A. the four dynasties (Shang, Zhou, Qin, Han)

   B. the three philosophies (Taoism, Legalism, and Confucianism)

   C. Buddhism religion

   D. common geographic features in China

2. Organize your podcast.

3. Write your podcast script.

4. Practice your podcast.

5. Present your podcast to your friends and instructor.

Alternative Assessment Rubric

Use the following rubric to grade your student's assessment.

	4	3	2	1	Points
Connection to the Chapter	The podcast includes all components and is connected to the chapter.	The podcast includes most components and is somewhat connected to the chapter.	The podcast includes some components and is somewhat connected to the chapter.	The podcast does not include any components and is not connected to the chapter.	
Creativity	The podcast is very creative and original.	The podcast is creative.	The podcast is somewhat creative.	The podcast is not creative.	
Organization	The podcast is organized and reads smoothly.	The podcast is mostly organized and reads somewhat smoothly.	The podcast is somewhat organized, but it does not read smoothly.	The podcast needs more organization and does not read smoothly.	
Grammar and Mechanics	There are no grammar and punctuation mistakes.	There are one or two grammar and punctuation mistakes.	There are several grammar and punctuation mistakes.	There are a distracting number of grammar and punctuation mistakes.	

Total Points _____/16

Average _____

Lesson Objectives

By the end of this lesson, your student will be able to:

- describe the location of places on a map using relative and exact location
- find the following locations on a map of Greece: Crete, Athens, and the Peloponnesus

Supporting Your Student

Explore

Help your student describe their location by starting at the global level. Remind them that they are on the planet Earth and live on a continent. Look at a map and help your student locate the continent they live on. Then, select the state, territory, or region of the country they live in. Next, identify the city or town they live in, followed by their neighborhood and street address.

Read (Greece on a Map)

Latitude and longitude may be a difficult concept for your student to grasp. Partner with them in reading the maps provided, discussing exact and relative location and how location impacts people. The people of ancient Greece were very close to water. How might that have affected their lives? Help your student use technology and/or tangible maps to explore the ideas of latitude, longitude, and relative location.

Practice

Your student may have trouble categorizing similarities and differences in the Venn diagram. Assist your student in completing the Venn diagram by asking questions about the previous section's learning such as "When we looked at the map of ancient Greece and its exact location, what did you notice?" and "When we looked at the map of ancient Greece and its relative location, what was similar and different?"

Learning Styles

Auditory learners may enjoy engaging in and listening to family conversations about how they use maps or relative and exact locations in their everyday lives.

Visual learners may enjoy scrutinizing the provided images/maps, using an online interactive map to explore Greece and the world at large, or using a tangible map to see latitude and longitude up close.

Kinesthetic learners may enjoy acting out exact locations. Plot out a simple grid using masking tape or another available material, making it workable for your space (i.e. an 8x8 grid). Give your student plot points to mark "locations" (i.e. latitude 6, longitude 4 is the movie theater). Alternatively, have your student design this grid.

Extension Activities

Artistic Representation of Greece

Print out a blank copy of the map of Greece and have your student use materials to "design" Greece. Their maps should include color and can use 3D materials (sequins for water, buttons for cities, or other materials as appropriate) to show the topography or areas of Greece. Your student can look up additional online maps to help with the creation of their map.

Creative Writing

Have your student write a short story about traveling around the world. Have them include descriptions of relative or exact location to identify the places they travel to.

Answer Key

Read *(Greece on a Map)*

Athens should be circled, Sparta should have a star next to it, and Crete should have a box around it. See picture for details.

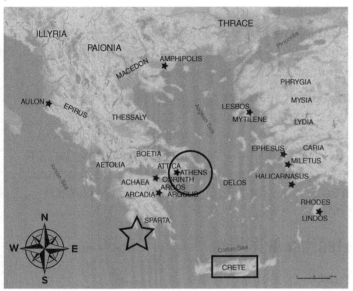

Practice

Relative Location

- describes a certain location by how it is spaced from another location in terms of distance, cost, or travel time
- does not use latitude and longitude
- very general

Both

- used by geographers
- describe the location of a place

Exact Location

- very specific
- uses the tools of latitude and longitude to identify where something is on the globe

Show What You Know

1. The Peloponnesian peninsula should be circled on the map. Athens, Sparta, and Crete should be labeled as seen on the map below.

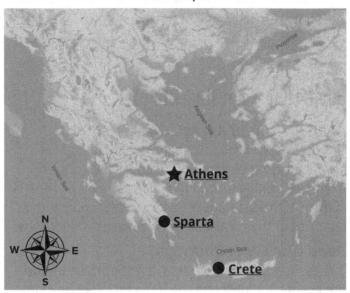

2. C
3. B
4. B

Lesson Objectives

By the end of this lesson, your student will be able to:

- compare and contrast the Minoans and Mycenaeans
- identify the beginning of the Greek Dark Age
- identify our source of information about the Greek Dark Age

Supporting Your Student

Read (Origins of Ancient Greece)
To best support your student, have them highlight key facts about each group in different colors. For example, highlight location and facts related to the culture of the Minoans in yellow and location and facts about the culture of the Mycenaeans in orange.

Read (The Greek Dark Age)
To best support your student, ask them to number the events and describe the progression of how the Greek Dark Age began, something that happened during the Dark Age, and how it ended.

Read (How We Know About the Greek Dark Age)
If your student is confused when working through this section, you could show them pictures of an archeological dig to help them better understand the process and what goes on when archeologists study ancient civilizations.

Learning Styles

Auditory learners may enjoy listening to ancient Greek language via an online dictionary or translator, discussing terminology and historical facts, and possibly listening to audiobooks that reference Greek culture.

Visual learners may enjoy exploration of maps, reading of books that reference Greek culture, or examining online timelines of ancient Greece.

Kinesthetic learners may enjoy creating and solving mazes, imagining how a Minotaur might move, and creating a volcano for your student to better understand the impact a volcano would have had on the people of ancient Greece. Directions can be found via an online search for creating an active volcano at home.

Extension Activities

Create
Have your student create a KWL chart. Use the KWL chart to log what they already know about ancient Greece and what they want to know about ancient Greece. The final column can be used for what they learn as they go through the unit.

Archeological Dig
Using whatever materials you deem appropriate (e.g., utensil, tool, or book), construct a dig site for your student. Place materials you choose within bags, and bury these in a small tub of sand and rock (or outside if you are adventurous). Your student should then excavate the site, logging each item as found and inferring what the item may have been used for in daily life. Encourage your student to think creatively and critically and have fun! Alternatively, excavation kits can be purchased online. Ask questions about the items found and what they could teach your student about the culture they are investigating.

Answer Key

Write *(What occurred during the Greek Dark Age, and how did it begin?)*

Answers will vary. Possible answer: Following the fall of the Mycenaeans from power, the Dark Age of Greece began. There was a lack of food and a decrease in population. Most information we have about the Dark Age is from archeologists who discovered burial sites from this time period. As the Dark Ages ended, the Archaic period began around 800 BC. Many Greek city-states gained power. Greek culture like philosophy and theater developed during this period.

Write *(How do we know about the Dark Age of Greece?)*

Answers will vary. Possible answer: Archeologists piece together ancient languages, artifacts, and ruins into information about people who lived a long time ago. We know about the Greek Dark Age because of archeologists' work. By studying ruins, artifacts, and tombs, archeologists have been able to paint a picture of what life was like during this time.

Show What You Know

1. Greek Dark Age
2. Archaic
3. Archeologists
4. tombs
5. Mycenaeans
6. Minoans
7. Answers will vary. Possible answer: The Minoans were believed to have lived primarily on the island of Crete, where remnants of a giant palace have been found. Between the years of 2600 BC and 1400 BC, this early Greek community thrived. They created language, art, and a vibrant culture. The city of Knossos was the most important place for the Minoans. The Mycenaeans were primarily located on the Peloponnesian peninsula mostly centered around a city named Mycenae. The Mycenaeans are credited with being the first to develop and speak the initial Greek language. The Mycenaeans were more aggressive and warlike than the Minoans. When they saw an opportunity to take over the rich, luxurious land of the Minoans, they took it! They both eventually lost power, and their civilizations declined, possibly because of a natural disaster.

Lesson Objectives

By the end of this lesson, your student will be able to:

- explain why the Classical Age of Greece is also called the Golden Age
- recognize Pericles's contributions to the Classical Age in Athens
- explain the influence of the land on Greek occupations

Supporting Your Student

In the Real World
Assist your student with making connections here. If possible, help connect your student to an architect. Help your student brainstorm questions, concerns, or ideas. Be present while your student conducts the interview. If an interview is not possible, help your student research online in effective ways.

Read (The Golden Age of Greece and Pericles)
This section contains a lot of difficult names to pronounce. It might be helpful to use your computer to get correct pronunciations if this is necessary. It also might be interesting to your student to look up some of the works created by the different people mentioned in this section of the text.

Write (Why was the Classical period described as golden? Cite evidence from the text to support your answer.)
Before beginning this task, discuss with your student what the term *golden* means to them. Then with that understanding and because this question requires your student to use evidence, it would be helpful to go back through the reading with a pencil or highlighter and find examples of things that qualify as golden. Once they have this compilation of evidence, they can begin writing an answer to the question.

Practice
This activity brings the lesson together. Make sure that your student understands what advantages and disadvantages are before they begin this assignment. Then help them understand that these would be things that line up with their likes and dislikes about where they live and how they live their life.

Online Connection
Journey with your student through research in this section. Whether in the local library, bookstore, or online, ensure alignment to lesson requirements. Discuss findings and talk about what these revelations mean in terms of culture and community. Perhaps consider partnering with your student and creating your own infographic of your hometown as you go.

Learning Styles

Auditory learners may enjoy talking through many of the sections in this lesson, including the Explore section. They may also enjoy listening to historical podcasts or books that reference Greek history.

Visual learners may enjoy creating models of Greek architecture.

Kinesthetic learners may enjoy acting out a scene from a Greek play. Preview the material to ensure it is age appropriate.

Extension Activities

Chef It Up
Have your student do some research online or in cookbooks about Greek food and popular recipes (stuffed grape leaves, gyros, Greek salad, spanakopita, tiropita). While discussing why these particular ingredients are associated with Greek cuisine, help your student cook the recipe and share with their family. If possible, plan a trip to a Greek restaurant and enjoy some of their delicacies.

Field Trip
With a parent or guardian, have your student venture down to their city's "agora" where their city's courthouse is located. Have them note what is around it. Are there parks, restaurants, churches, or stores like in a Greek city-state? Have them sketch what they see, take comparison notes, or use a camera to document their experience. Discuss what is similar about a modern agora compared to one in ancient Greece.

Answer Key

Write *(Why was the Classical period described as golden? Cite evidence from the text to support your answer.)*

Answers will vary. Possible answer: Once politicians introduced democracy and city-states rose up, Greek people were very successful. During this time, Athens and Sparta fought and defeated the Persian Empire in a great war. The Parthenon was built. Socrates and Hippocrates were making names for themselves. They built large theaters, and Euripides and Sophocles wrote great tragedies. Finally, Pythagoras, the great mathematician, lived during the Classical Age.

Practice

Answers will vary. Possible answers:

Advantages might include: the development of democracy, art, architecture, fishing farming, mining

Disadvantages might include: war, trade introducing enemies, Athens becoming too powerful

Show What You Know
1. False
2. False
3. False
4. True
5. False
6. True
7. False
8. True
9. False
10. True

Lesson Objectives

By the end of this lesson, your student will be able to:

- identify reasons Greece had city-state governments rather than a central government
- trace the development of Athens from an oligarchy to a democracy
- identify major philosophers of ancient Athens and describe the important teachings of each

Supporting Your Student

Write *(What are two reasons why Greece had city-state governments rather than a central government?)*
In this section, support your student by giving them a highlighter or a yellow crayon to go back in the text and look for specific examples of why Greece formed city-states. Direct them to read the second paragraph of Read (City-States of Greece).

Read *(History of Athens)*
In this section, it may be helpful to look over the timeline with your student. Discuss features such as the key, the meaning of each color, the years, and the arrow at the end. If they are unfamiliar with dates written as BC, explain what this stands for and how it was used.

Also in this section, have them search for the bold keywords and reference the timeline to place the government systems chronologically as they read.

Write *(Fill in the chart below to summarize the philosophy of the three Greek philosophers.)*
For this section, direct your student to the Read (Philosophers of Athens) page, which has a paragraph on each of the three philosophers. It may be helpful for them to fill in the chart for each philosopher as they read the corresponding paragraph rather than to go back at the end and write about each person.

Online Connection
For this extension activity, assist your student in searching for some age-appropriate philosophers of today. Search digital platforms such as YouTube or TIME for Kids to seek thinkers of the current era who your student may share values with. Help them make connections between the views of the philosopher and their personal values.

Learning Styles

Auditory learners may enjoy videos on ancient Greek democracy and philosophers, land and architecture, and the political process in various city-states. Podcasts may be available citing similar history.

Visual learners may enjoy studying the geography of ancient Greece to learn more about the various mountain ranges, islands, and physical barriers that separated city-states from one another.

Kinesthetic learners may enjoy constructing an agora from household materials or recreating the Greek coastal region featuring Athens.

Extension Activities

Create
Have your student construct a replica of an Athenian agora where democratic representatives would have met. Help your student research and, find household materials, and guide your student through the architectural process of construction.

Further Research
Provide the opportunity for your student to perform more in-depth research about the Greek philosophers. Your student can use the public library or online resources to create a set of biographical notes depicting more details about these three men's lives.

Government and Philosophy in Ancient Greece

Answer Key

Write *(What are two reasons why Greece had city-state governments rather than a central government?)*

Answers will vary. Possible answers: The geography of Greece had too many physical barriers. The wealthy population in Greece enjoyed their independence and wanted to maintain that to the best of their ability.

Write *(Fill in the chart to summarize the philosophy of the three Greek philosophers.)*

Answers will vary. Possible answers:

Socrates	Plato	Aristotle
first philosopher created Socratic method philosophy of politics good vs. evil	student of Socrates how humans adapt to change believed in equal classes	student of Plato interested in science logic, reason, and self-control create wisdom

Show What You Know

1. E
2. C
3. A
4. B
5. D
6. C
7. A
8. B
9. D
10. Answers will vary. Possible answer: Plato was a student of Socrates. His philosophy focused on the human ability to adapt to change and the meaning of life. He believed that there was a role for everyone in society.

Lesson Objectives

By the end of this lesson, your student will be able to:

- identify key features of Spartan culture
- compare and contrast the lives of Greeks in Athens and Sparta
- compare education in Ancient Greece with education today

Supporting Your Student

Read (Life in Sparta)

In this section, it may be helpful to give your student a highlighter to help them select key ideas about life in Sparta. Direct them toward adjectives that will help them in the following Write section where they will choose five words to describe life in Sparta.

Write (What is one way the city-states of Athens and Sparta are the same? What is one way they are different?)

For this activity, it may be helpful to have your student answer the question as they are reading through the text on page 4. If they require further assistance, you can read the "Sparta vs. Athens" section aloud to them as they record the similarities and differences.

Practice

In this section, you can support your learner by reading through and pointing out elements of ancient Greek education that are similar to their education today. Direct them to paragraph one in the section "Education in Ancient Greece" to look for similar subject matters that were studied. Direct them to paragraph four in the same section to look for gender equality in education.

Learning Styles

Auditory learners may enjoy listening to the sounds of a flute or harp, traditional instruments in ancient Greece, while they work.

Visual learners may enjoy using two different colors of highlighters. This may help them organize their ideas before answering the question.

Kinesthetic learners may enjoy acting out a scene from a traditional Athenian play. Search online for some ideas. Kinesthetic learners may also enjoy creating their own "Spartan Race" with obstacles along the course.

Extension Activities

DIY Spartan Race

Have your student create a Spartan race in their backyard or at their local playground. Spartan races are running races that typically have 20 obstacles for a 5K race, but they can make the race as long or as short as they wish. Maybe the obstacles involve hopscotch, jumping over a log, or climbing across the monkey bars. They could even make an obstacle out of a cardboard box. Use what they have to create a fun Spartan race.

Spartan School Field Day

For one day, have your student pretend they attend school in Sparta. Fill their day with plenty of exercise, a little reading and writing, and more exercise! Be sure they stay hydrated during this day of athletic fun. Look up traditional field day games and activities for some fun ideas.

Answer Key

Write *(Choose five words that best describe life in Sparta.)*
Answers will vary. Possible answers: bravery, strength, discipline, endurance, warriors

Write *(What is one way the city-states of Athens and Sparta are the same? What is one way they are different?)*
Answers will vary. Possible answers:

Athens: military was optional, people enjoyed luxuries and fancy foods, focus on art and education, mainly democratic government

Sparta: two kings, military focus, women treated as equals, slaves were rebellious

Both: had a government, most powerful city-states in Greece, had slaves

Practice
Answers will vary. Possible answers: In Athens, students studied literature, science, math, politics, music, and art. In Sparta, boys and girls both attended school.

Show What You Know
1. military
2. discipline
3. kings
4. Sparta
5. Athens
6. citizens
7. girls
8. Leonidas I
9. warriors
10. Answers will vary. Possible answer: In my opinion, I would rather attend school in Sparta. First, I'm a girl, so I would like to be able to attend school. Next, I think the military is important. Last, I would like to learn how to fight in order to defend my family and my community. For these reasons, I would choose to attend school in Sparta.

Greek Literature and Mythology

Lesson Objectives

By the end of this lesson, your student will review the following big ideas from Chapter 5.

- describe Homer's contributions to literature
- distinguish between genres of Greek literature, including epics, fables, plays, and myths
- explain how the Greek belief in gods influenced the people's lives
- analyze the lasting appeal of the Greek myths

Supporting Your Student

Read *(Greek Mythology)*

In this section, encourage connections to prior knowledge by asking if your student has ever seen references to any of the figures in Greek mythology in current culture. For example, the Percy Jackson series is about Greek mythology.

Write *(What contributes to the lasting appeal of Greek mythology?)*

For this section, you can support your student by directing them to the first and second paragraphs in the "Greek Mythology" section. Ask, "Why are people still interested in the stories told in Greek mythology?" to help them analyze the lasting appeal of these myths.

Show What You Know

Highlight key terms or phrases in this section to help your student determine the literary genre. Phrases to highlight are as follows:

1. Odysseus, on his journey home to Ithaca
2. traditional tale, goddesses
3. comedy, the funniest scene
4. "The Ants and The Grasshopper"

Learning Styles

Auditory learners may enjoy listening to different readings of Greek literature, such as Aesop's Fables or a child-friendly version of popular Greek myths.

Visual learners may enjoy watching a movie with characters from ancient Greek mythology. There are many child-friendly options.

Kinesthetic learners may enjoy acting out a fable, myth, or play. "The Frogs" is a play that has child-friendly scripts available online.

Extension Activities

Greek Mythology Diorama

Have your student create a diorama depicting an ancient Greek myth. Use an old shoebox to display the setting. Have them build characters out of modeling clay, cardboard, or any other craft supplies you have at home. Using their diorama as a prop, have them retell the myth in their own words.

Beast Pictionary

Without showing them a picture, choose one mythological beast and describe this beast in detail. Have your student try to draw what they think the beast looks like. When they are finished with their drawing, show them the picture of the beast you were describing. Does their illustration look similar to the picture? Next, switch roles and have your student describe a beast for you to draw!

Answer Key

Practice

Answers will vary. Possible answers:

Epics: lengthy narrative poems, stories about heroes, examples are the Iliad and the Odyssey

Fables: short stories about animals, examples are Aesop's Fables and "The Tortoise and the Hare"

Plays: performed in theaters; entertainment; comedy, satyr, and tragedy

Myths: traditional sacred stories, gods and goddesses

Write *(What contributes to the lasting appeal of Greek mythology?)*

Answers will vary. Possible answer: Greek Mythology has lasting appeal because it provides entertainment but also teaches valuable lessons. The characters are relatable because they make mistakes and overcome problems. The stories and lessons learned in myths are still relevant today.

Write *(How did the poet Homer contribute to Greek culture and society?)*

Answers will vary. Possible answer: Homer wrote two famous Greek epics, *The Iliad* and *The Odyssey*. These epics provided Greeks with a common set of values to reference and distinguish right from wrong. His poems provided an example of heroism, nobility, and what it means to live a good life.

Show What You Know

1. D
2. A
3. C
4. B
5. D
6. B
7. D
8. C

Greek Language, Math, and Science

Lesson Objectives

By the end of this lesson, your student will be able to:

- recognize the importance of the Greek language and its connection to other languages
- describe the accomplishments of Greece's prominent figures in math and science
- recognize Greek contributions to music, art, and architecture

Supporting Your Student

Explore

Other Greek roots are *anthro,* meaning "human," *aqu,* meaning "water," *byss,* meaning "bottom," and *chrome,* meaning "color." It would be helpful to look up more words with Greek roots to give your student further examples. Ask them if knowing the root meanings would help them define an unknown word. This guiding question will help your student better understand the importance of the Greek language.

Take a Closer Look *(Compare and Contrast)*

For this activity, your student needs to look at the English and Greek alphabets. Have them look at each as a whole. Ask, "How many letters does each have? What do you notice?" Then go letter by letter to compare. Ask them which letters look the same and which look different. These steps will help them compare and contrast the two alphabets.

Read *(Greece's Prominent Figures in Math and Science)*

Before beginning this section, create a chart with six columns. Label each column with one of the following titles: Pythagoras, Euclid, Archimedes, Thales of Miletus, Aristotle, and Hypatia. Then as your student reads, have them fill out each person's accomplishments and contributions to math and science.

Read *(Greek Contribution to Art, Music, Sports, and Architecture)*

It would be helpful to have your student research different art from ancient Greece. Also, you might show your student various examples of temple columns from different orders. These examples will give your student real-life references and help them better understand the concepts.

Learning Styles

Auditory learners may enjoy a podcast or audiobook describing the three different orders and their unique architectural details. They may also enjoy discussing the reasons why the Greek language is essential.

Visual learners may enjoy photos of architecture and various Greek inventions like the compound pulley.

Kinesthetic learners may enjoy creating models of the different columns. They may also enjoy creating words and sentences using the Greek alphabet.

Extension Activities

Create a Greek Temple

Using clay, have your student create a temple using the examples from the worktext. Prompt them to choose which order they want to imitate with their columns and create a miniature temple. When done, they can paint it.

Biography

Direct your student to research one of the Greek figures from the worktext. Have them write a short biography about the chosen figure's life events, accomplishments, and family. They can also add photos to the biography if that helps them better understand their chosen figure and associated accomplishments.

Answer Key

Explore

1. <u>anti</u>biotic
2. <u>hydr</u>ation
3. <u>gram</u>mar
4. <u>bio</u>hazard
5. <u>biblio</u>graphy
6. <u>hydr</u>aulics
7. <u>doc</u>trine
8. <u>geo</u>logy

Write (Summarize in your own words the importance of the Greek language and how it connects to other languages.)

Answers will vary. Possible answer: The Greek language contains written accounts of history. Also, the language helped spread religions such as Christianity through its spoken and written word. Many science-related words are of Greek origin as well since many English words' roots are derived from Greek.

Write (What is one accomplishment of Thales of Miletus?)

Answers will vary. Possible answer: Thales was the first individual to whom mathematical discovery was attributed. He is best known for using geometry to determine the heights of the pyramids and the distance of the ships from shore.

Show What You Know

1. B
2. C
3. A
4. C
5. A
6. D
7. Answers will vary. Possible answer: The Greek language is connected to other languages because many words originate from it.

Lesson Objectives

By the end of this lesson, your student will be able to:

- identify the traits that made Alexander the Great a unique leader
- explain the reason for the spread of Hellenistic culture
- identify influences of ancient Greece seen today

Supporting Your Student

Explore

After reading the section review, revisit the concepts learned throughout the chapter about ancient Greece. The ideas about ancient Greek culture will help your student create captions for the pictures. This activity is to connect past learning to this lesson.

Read (Alexander the Great)

During the reading of this section, it would be helpful for your student to compile a list of the leadership characteristics that Alexander the Great had. This list will help them when answering the question at the end of the section.

Read (Greek Influence)

It would be helpful to look up other examples of how Greek culture affects us today. For example, many colleges have sororities or use Greek names. Another example could be how many medical and scientific terms are derived from the Greek language.

Learning Styles

Auditory learners may enjoy listening to Greek poems and having plays read aloud to them. They may also enjoy discussing with their instructor key reasons for the spread of Hellenic culture.

Visual learners may enjoy art and images from the Hellenic period. They may also enjoy studying maps of the empire Alexander the Great ruled and how the land was divided into dynasties following his death.

Kinesthetic learners may enjoy acting out Greek plays. They may also enjoy creating Greek-inspired art.

Extension Activities

Poster

Have your student create a poster all about Alexander the Great. Have them include images of sculptures of Alexander, facts about his life, and his accomplishments. Have them expand on the information from the worktext by researching Alexander's life and legacy.

Flowchart

Have your student create a flowchart of events from Alexander the Great's ascension to power to the spread of Hellenic culture. Have them include images and explanations of how the circumstances led to the spread of Hellenic culture.

Answer Key

Explore

Answers will vary. Possible answers:

1. The Old Testament was translated from Hebrew to Greek, then to many other languages.

2. The Greek language influenced many other languages.

3. Women during the Hellenic period discussing the arts

Write *(What is one attribute Alexander the Great had as a leader?)*

Answers will vary. Possible answers: Alexander the Great led by example. He was on the front line and experienced what his troops did. Alexander the Great used speed and surprise to help him win battles. Alexander the Great understood his opponents.

Write *(What is one area of our daily lives that the ancient Greeks influenced?)*

Answers will vary. Possible answers: The Greeks influenced the geometry we use today. The ancient Greeks influenced and contributed to astronomy. The Greek theater influences many films.

Show What You Know

1. B
2. C
3. trade
4. theater
5. modern
6. Macedonia
7. Answers will vary. Possible answers: The Greeks influenced the math that we use today. The ancient Greeks influenced and contributed to astronomy. Many films are influenced by Greek theater.

Lesson Objectives

By the end of this lesson, your student will review the following big ideas from Chapter 7.

- Crete, Athens, and the Peloponnesus can be found on a map of Ancient Greece. (Lesson 39)
- There are both similarities between the Minoans and Mycenaeans, such as their art, language, and location. (Lesson 40)
- In the classical Greek era, the land influenced occupations. (Lesson 41)
- Greece's city-state governments became a democracy. (Lesson 42)
- Sparta and Athens had some similarities but were also very different from one another, mainly as a result of the values and philosophies of their governments. (Lesson 43)
- The Greeks introduced four main genres of literature: epics, fables, plays, and myths. (Lesson 44)
- Prominent figures in ancient Greece made many important contributions to language, math, science, art, and sports. (Lesson 45)
- Alexander the Great was the leader of the largest ancient empire, and his influence caused the spread of Hellenistic culture. (Lesson 46)

Supporting Your Student

Review *(Early Civilizations of Ancient Greece)*
It would be helpful to compare the two early civilizations. Ask your student how they were the same and how they were different.

Review *(Greece's Classical Era)*
After reading this review, discuss with your student how Pericles contributed to the evolution of the Greek government during the Classical Era of Greece. It would be helpful to create a graphic connecting Peciles to milestones in the Greek government.

Take a Closer Look *(Greek Beliefs)*
For this section, it would be helpful for your student to understand that in Greek belief, Zeus rules all the other gods and goddesses. In contrast, Christianity believes in one all-powerful God. The Greek gods each had individual powers rather than being all-powerful.

Practice *(Debate)*
Your student may find it helpful to first focus on all the positives that came from the spread of the Hellenic culture. Then have your student create an argument for why it was good for the ancient world. Afterward the student will do the same thing but with the negatives. It would also be helpful to engage in verbal debate, so you may want to debate with your student.

Learning Styles

Auditory learners may enjoy debating the pros and cons of the spread of Hellenic culture. They may also enjoy creating a podcast discussing the various civilizations of Greece, such as the Minoans and the Mycenaeans, and the Spartans and Athenians.

Visual learners may enjoy creating a timeline of events from early Greek civilizations to the Hellenic culture spreading. They may also enjoy looking at artifacts from ancient Greece either in museums if accessible or online.

Kinesthetic learners may enjoy creating models of various columns from different orders, such as the Ionic, Doric, and Corinthians. They may also enjoy acting out different myths from Greek mythology.

Extension Activities

Compare and Contrast
Have your student compare and contrast the various periods of ancient Greece. What characteristics do these periods share? How do these times differ from each other? Things to think about include their beliefs, jobs, wars, and leaders. Here are the different times:

- Early ancient Greece (origin)
- Greek Dark Ages
- Archaic period
- Classical Age of Greece
- Hellenistic

Virtual Field Trip

Have your student go on a virtual field trip to Greece. The British Museum's website offers free virtual tours of the temples. Another resource for virtual tours is Clio Muse Tours. They have a wide selection of countries to tour online.

Answer Key

Write *(What type of government did the classical age introduce to Greece?)*

Answers will vary. Possible answer: They introduced democracy and city-states.

Write *(How did the spread of the Greek language help the ancient world? What led to the spread of Hellenic culture?)*

Answers will vary. Possible answers: The spread of the Greek language made it easier to communicate and share ideas with other cultures. The spread of Hellenic culture occurred because of trade expansion and because the land conquered by Alexander the Great was split up into dynasties.

Practice *(Three's a Crowd)*

1. Diadochi; Ionic and Doric are orders of Greece, but Diadochi are generals.

2. Hellenic; Epics and fables are both types of Greek literature, but Hellenic is a culture and does not belong.

3. Corinthian order; Minoans and Mycenaeans are two early Greek civilizations. The Corinthian order is not an early civilization.

4. deities; Deities do not belong because idioms and plays are both parts of literature.

5. labyrinth; Labyrinth because it is a maze, and the Archaic period and the Dark Ages of Greece refer to times.

Drawings will vary based on the group of words they choose.

Practice *(Create Your Own Greek Literature)*

Answers will vary depending on what type of literature your student chooses.

Practice *(Debate)*

Answers will vary. Possible answers:

Argument for the Spread of Hellenic Culture: The spread of the Hellenic culture allowed for cultures shared and a more widely known language. This spread of culture and language allowed for new ideas to be shared. This was also when the Bible was translated into Greek, and the New Testament was written in Greek.

Argument Against the Spread of Hellenic Culture: The Hellenic culture spreading was not helpful for the ancient world because it forced Greek culture on other groups of people. Some traditions were lost, and in some dynasties, different cultures and religions were not as tolerated.

Quick Review

Refer to the statement your student circled in the Show What You Know section to self-assess their knowledge of the chapter concepts. Then to assist in determining if your student is ready to take the assessment, consider:

- Having your student identify key locations of ancient Greece on the map.
- Having your student explain the similarities and differences of the early Greek civilizations.
- Having your student describe the different time eras of ancient Greece.
- Having your student discuss preeminent figures of ancient Greece.
- Having your student explain the importance of the Greek language.
- Having your student describe how the Hellenic culture spread and its effects.
- Having your student identify how Greek culture influences life today.

Chapter Assessment

Use the words in the Word Bank to complete the sentences. Not all words will be used.

Word Bank: Pericles   Dark   early
deities   Classical   military
politically   epic   Ionic
Minoans

1. The Minoans and the Mycenaeans were two _____ Greek civilizations.

2. The Odyssey is an example of an _____ Greek literature.

3. The _____ Age of Greece introduced democracy, and city-states rose up.

4. There was a lack of food and a decrease in population during the _____ Age of Greece.

5. Athens focused on the arts and education, while Sparta's focus was primarily on the _____.

6. The Greek dynasties during the Hellenistic period were not united _____.

Circle the correct answer.

7. What does Hellenism mean?

   A. the historical spread of ancient Asian culture, religion, and language over foreign peoples conquered by the Asian Empires

   B. the historical spread of ancient Egyptian culture, religion, and language over foreign peoples conquered by Egypt

   C. the historical spread of ancient Greek culture, religion, and language over foreign peoples conquered by Greeks

   D. the historical spread of ancient Roman culture, religion, and language over foreign peoples conquered by Romans

8. Athens was known as the birthplace of _____.

   A. democracy

   B. monopoly

   C. oligarchy

   D. Acropolis

9. What is one trait that made Alexander the Great a successful leader?

   A. He was very strict with his people.

   B. He forced everyone to have the same customs.

   C. He led by example.

   D. He was not successful.

Discover! SOCIAL STUDIES • GRADE 6 • CHAPTER 7 ASSESSMENT

143

Answer the following questions in complete sentences.

10. How did ancient Greece influence modern times?

....

....

....

....

....

....

11. Compare and contrast the Minoan and the Mycenaean civilizations.

....

....

....

....

....

....

12. Compare education in Athens with today's education.

....

....

....

....

....

....

Chapter Assessment Answer Key

1. early
2. epic
3. Classical
4. Dark
5. military
6. politically
7. C
8. A
9. C
10. Answers will vary. Possible answer: The Greeks influenced the math that we use today. The ancient Greeks influenced and contributed to astronomy. Many films are influenced by Greek theater. Also, it was the birthplace of democracy which is used today.
11. Answers will vary. Possible answers: The Minoans lived on the island of Crete. They created a writing system, art, and vibrant culture. Mycenaeans were from the Peloponnesian peninsula and more violent than the Minoans and more ruthless. They conquered the Minoans and used their art, writing, and customs, forming Greek civilization.
12. Answers will vary. Possible answers: The purpose of education today as in Athens is to produce good citizens who contribute to society. Also, both started school around six. They differ in that girls in Athens did not typically attend a school where they do today.

Alternative Assessment

Project: Magazine Article

Project Requirements or Steps:

For this project, design a magazine article that addresses an issue discussed in the unit. If needed, research some relevant and recent issues that can be written about from your perspective.

Include the following elements in the magazine article.

- A title or headline
- A date
- Sources
- A fluid and intriguing progression of the subject and writing

Alternative Assessment Rubric

Use the following rubric to grade your student's assessment.

	4	3	2	1	Points
Research	The magazine article provides detailed and factual information and the topic is thoroughly researched.	The magazine article has some detailed and factual information and the topic is thoroughly researched.	The magazine article has very little detailed information and the topic is not thoroughly researched.	The magazine article does not provide detailed and factual information and the topic is not thoroughly researched.	
Perspective and Interest	The magazine article provides a unique perspective on the topic, and the writing is well-developed.	The magazine article provides a unique perspective on the topic, but the writing could be more well-developed.	The magazine article provides very little unique perspective on the topic, and the writing is not well-developed.	The magazine article does not provide a unique perspective on the topic, and the writing is not well-developed.	
Required Elements	The magazine article makes clear and repetitive connections to the chapter and includes all the required elements.	The magazine article is related to the chapter but does not include all required elements.	The magazine article makes one or two references to the chapter but does not include all required elements.	The magazine article is unrelated to the chapter and does not include all required elements.	
Grammar and Mechanics	The magazine article has no grammar issues and uses advanced vocabulary.	The magazine article contains a few grammar mistakes and uses age-appropriate vocabulary.	The magazine article contains several grammar mistakes and uses age-appropriate vocabulary.	The magazine article contains a distracting number of grammar mistakes and overly-simplified vocabulary.	

Total Points _____/16

Average _____

Discover! SOCIAL STUDIES • GRADE 6 • CHAPTER 7 ASSESSMENT

147

Lesson Objectives

By the end of this lesson, your student will be able to:

- identify and describe places in Italy and surrounding countries on a map
- describe the geographic features of Italy
- identify the earliest inhabitants of Italy and their contributions

Supporting Your Student

Take a Closer Look

This section is used to activate prior knowledge while opening up the lesson about a new topic. Your student who struggles with listing what they see, think, and wonder can be prompted with questions. Ask your student, "What do you see in the photo?" and "What is the image showing you about Italy?" You can help your student by saying, "I see a large body of water and mountains surrounding the country. I wonder if people live in the mountains." After providing your student with something you see, prompt them to find something they see. Then, ask them to think about a question related to what they just described. At the end of the lesson, come back to these questions to see if they have been answered or can be used as a springboard for further research.

Explore

During this section, your student will look closely at the picture that says "ITALY." In each letter, they will notice a geographical feature or landmark in Italy. Guide your student by asking, "What predictions can you make about Italy based on the image?" If they are struggling, model letter I for them. You can start by saying, "In letter I, we see a tall landmark. It may be a building, but it looks more like a statue. What are some of the features of the landmark? It has a lot of square cutouts and it almost looks like it is leaning!" Ask your student if they can do the same with the letter T. Ask your student to make observations as well as predictions based on the image by saying, "What do you think we will see when we explore Italy?"

Write *(What is one benefit of Italy being a peninsula?)*

Help your student to see the benefit of being surrounded by water. Ask them to think about what water is used for. Maybe suggest to them that it provides drinking water as an initial suggestion to prompt them. See if they can think about the needs of a country. Also, talk to them about what it is like when they play a game where they have to plan a strategy against someone else. Ask them if it is important to be able to see things from all around them when defending their strategy. Help them to see that being on a peninsula is like that—you can see all around you and defend from all sides.

Write *(If you could visit one place in Italy, what would it be? Why?)*

Your student may struggle with deciding on a place to visit in Italy or coming up with a reason why. In addition to looking at the places you have discussed in the lesson, you could talk about other places in Italy you know about or seek out other resources to find places to visit.

Practice

To assist your student in completing the activity, point to the map. Ask your student to identify the surrounding countries by touching them and saying their names. The second question requires your student to understand the geographical features of a map and to compare Italy to its surrounding countries. Refer to the water and ask your student to list the bodies of water that the countries share with Italy. This leads into the last question. After repeated exposure to the benefits of a peninsula, your student should be able to understand that water provides a lot of economic benefits, such as trade and transport. If your student struggles with this, start a discussion about the way goods can be transported from place to place.

Italy and Its Geographic Features

Learning Styles

Auditory learners may enjoy listening to Italian songs to gain a deeper understanding of the culture.

Visual learners may enjoy searching for more pictures of Italy on a search engine and making a digital scrapbook of places, landmarks, and geographic features.

Kinesthetic learners may enjoy using their body to create some of the geographical features of Italy, such as the mountains or bodies of water. For example, they might get on their hands and knees on the ground and round their back to look like a tall mountain.

Extension Activities

Etruscans Research
Have your student look up additional information about the Etruscans, the second group to inhabit Italy. Then, have them create a brochure about who they were and their contributions to Italy, including specific details from their findings.

Write a Story
Have your student imagine they just landed in Italy. They could write a short story about their adventures in Italy. They should include the geographic features and important places mentioned in the lessons. For example, perhaps the characters in the story could visit them or these locations create a backdrop for the action that happens in the story. What would happen if the Leaning Tower of Pisa fell?

Answer Key

Explore
Answers may vary. Possible answers: Italy has tall towers, colorful buildings, and different bodies of water.

Write *(What is one benefit of Italy being a peninsula?)*
Answers may vary. Possible answers: trade, travel, transport of goods, recreation, fishing, defense

Write *(If you could visit one place in Italy, what would it be? Why?)*
Answers may vary. Possible answer: I would like to visit Rome because it is Italy's largest city and Vatican City has a lot of great art.

Practice
1. Answers may vary. Possible answers:
   - France, Switzerland, Austria, Slovenia
   - They are all near bodies of water. Some of the bodies of water they are near are the Mediterranean Sea, Adriatic Sea, Ionian Sea, Tyrrhenian Sea, and Ligurian Sea.
   - economic (fishing), trade, transport, travel, recreation, defense

Show What You Know
2. A: Mediterranean Sea
   F: Apennine Mountains
   E: Alps
   B: Switzerland
   C: France
   D: Austria
3. Answers may vary. Possible answers: Rome is the capital and largest city. Venice is built right on the ocean and has many canals for people to travel by boat.
4. Answers may vary. Possible answers: Advantages of living on a peninsula are opportunities for trade, travel, transportation, and defense of the country.
5. A, C
6. A, D

Lesson Objectives

By the end of this lesson, your student will be able to:

- describe the governing branches of the Roman Republic
- analyze the pros and cons of the ancient Roman government on various groups
- describe the significance of the Law of the Twelve Tables
- identify the First Triumvirate
- describe the transition of Rome from a Republic to an Empire

Supporting Your Student

Explore

Support your student by asking guiding questions like, "Can you think of any groups or organizations that support causes in our community?," "Who is our mayor?," and "How is the mayor elected?" If your student does not know the answer, encourage them to research their community to find out and report back.

Read (The Government of the Roman Republic)

Your student may not fully grasp the concept of due process. Support your student by offering examples to further explain the concept. You might say, "Due process means that the government has to follow the rules to find someone guilty of breaking the law," or "Have you ever heard a police officer say, 'You have the right to remain silent?' on TV? Letting an arrested person know what rights they have is part of due process."

Write (Identify three causes of tensions in Rome during the Republic.)

Help your student make deeper connections to the material by asking them to imagine life in the Roman Republic. Exercising an empathetic approach to understanding this time in history will make the content more relevant for your student. You can ask guiding questions like, "If you were a plebeian earning a decent living for your work and your work was taken away because enslaved people were forced to do it

without payment, how would you feel?" or "Can you imagine why it was easy for generals to gain power by making people feel more divided? How do you think that worked?"

Learning Styles

Auditory learners may enjoy hearing speeches from Julius Caesar or Augustus. Look up some videos where you can hear their speeches being performed by actors.

Visual learners may enjoy looking at sculptures and architecture created during the Roman Republic.

Kinesthetic learners may enjoy acting out the process of creating a law the way the Romans did. Guide your student to think of a new rule and consequence they would want to implement at home. Allow your student to gather other "citizens" of your household to hold a vote on whether the new "law" should be enacted or not.

Extension Activities

Roles in Rome

Your student should consider what worked in the Roman Republic and what was less successful. Have them create a pros and cons list for the government of the Roman Republic.

Virtual Field Trip

Search online for virtual field trips of Roman ruins. After viewing one (or more), ask your student to visualize themselves in that place and time in the world. Have them describe what they think it would have been like in some way.

Answer Key

Explore

Answers will vary depending on where your student lives. Review your student's response to ensure that they have understood how their chosen leader obtained their position.

In the Real World (*Creating Rules*)

Answers will vary based on what law your student proposes. Make sure your student's response is well-reasoned.

Write (*Summarize one way that the government under the Republic differed from the Period of Kings.*)

Answers will vary. Possible answer: The Roman Republic was different from the Roman monarchy because the Republic had many leaders who shared the power rather than just one ruler. Under the Republic, the consuls, magistrates, senate, and the assemblies all had some power over what happened in Rome, while a Roman king was the chief executive, military leader, high priest, and judge for the whole kingdom.

Write (*Identify three causes of tensions in Rome during the Republic.*)

Answers will vary. Possible answer: Enslaved laborers did work that plebeians had previously been paid to do, reducing the economic opportunities of plebeians. There was a division in factions as to who supported societal changes in order to balance out the inequality. Several revolts were staged. Military generals furthered divisions for personal gain.

Show What You Know

1. A
2. C
3. B
4. E
5. F
6. D
7. True
8. First: Caesar, Pompey, Crassus
   Second: Octavian, Antony, Lepidus
9. Answers will vary. Possible answer: There was a lot of conflict in the Roman Republic, which led to the First Triumvirate. When Caesar was killed, Octavian and the Second Triumvirate claimed all of the power.

Lesson Objectives

By the end of this lesson, your student will be able to:

- examine the examine the roles of different groups in ancient Rome
- describe how conquered people and lands were integrated into ancient Roman society
- describe the religious views of ancient Rome and how they changed over time

Supporting Your Student

Create

In this section, your student will pick a subgroup of ancient Roman society that they will study throughout the lesson. As the lesson progresses, have discussions with your student about what information would be useful to know in order to write a story about their group. This can include their home lives, their jobs in society, their economic status, their political powers, and their status in relation to other groups. They can choose to write a narrative, a journal entry, a song, or a few short paragraphs. Remind your student to write from the point of view of someone in the group. For example, "I was in town today and I saw a freedman..." Throughout their story, your student should demonstrate to the reader what life was like for that particular group in ancient Rome.

Write *(What were the differences between each social class?)*

Your student may struggle to identify the overarching differences between the social classes. Discuss each class with your student to help them summarize what made someone fit into a specific class. Ask your student to identify aspects of each class that made it unique. It may help your student to list these elements on paper to help them visualize the differences. Remind your student that there are a few differences that separated each of the classes.

Write *(Identify two ways life for women in Rome changed after the Republic.)*

Your student may struggle to identify ways conquered people impacted the Roman Empire. Ask your student what happened after a new group of people was conquered by the Romans. Review the information from the previous lesson regarding the influx of enslaved people into the Republic and how it caused tension for plebeians. Consider asking some follow up questions such as, "What did the Romans expect from conquered people?" and "Why would they want these things?" These questions should guide your student in their writing.

Learning Styles

Auditory learners may enjoy listening to stories of daily life for the different classes in ancient Roman society.

Visual learners may enjoy drawing a pyramid diagram to organize the social classes in order.

Kinesthetic learners may enjoy playing social class charades by acting out different social classes in ancient Rome and having you guess the correct answer (and vice versa).

Extension Activities

Draw

Have your student create a comic strip of a day in the life of one of the social classes in ancient Rome. They should have at least six panels with visuals, captions at the bottom, and context from the lesson.

Pros and Cons

Have your student imagine they were part of a group of people being conquered by the Romans. They should make a pros and cons list of the good and bad things that would come with being conquered by the Roman Empire.

Answer Key

Explore

Answers will vary based on your student's observations about roles and class in their life. Review their answers to make sure their connections are logical. Possible answers for jobs include doctor, lawyer, mechanic, teacher, business owner, factory worker, or retail salesperson. Possible answers for homes include houses, apartments, condominiums, and townhouses.

Write *(What were the differences between each social class?)*

Answers will vary. Possible answers: Each social class was separated by wealth, job, and status in society. The higher classes had more money, government-related jobs, and were regarded as important while the lower classes had less money, more labor-focused jobs, and were not thought to be important.

Write *(Identify two ways life for women in Rome changed after the Republic.)*

Answers will vary. Possible answers might focus on women owning businesses and girls being encouraged to gain an education.

Show What You Know

1. 3: Plebeian
   4: Freedmen
   1: Patrician
   2: Equite
   5: Enslaved

2. False

3. B

4. Answers will vary. Possible answer: Roman religion started with many gods that were adopted from the Greeks, but eventually most Romans followed Christianity.

5. Answers will vary. Possible answers: The patricians were consuls or senators and had great power and influence in society. The equites were also important in the government because they were originally part of the Roman cavalry. The plebeians were workers and sometimes served in the assemblies and helped to create laws. The freedmen were former slaves who worked for wages. The enslaved people had no rights and received no money for their work.

6. Answers will vary. Possible answers: The Romans expanded by conquering other empires, which helped their military grow.

Lesson Objectives

By the end of this lesson, your student will be able to:

- examine the expansive trade routes of the Roman Empire
- identify key trade regions and the goods that were bought and sold
- examine ways that the Romans changed transportation
- explain the purpose and importance of the Roman roads

Supporting Your Student

Online Connection (Roads)

In this section, your student is required to research a road in their area. Your student may struggle to get started with selecting a street or may not know where to start with their research. Consider pulling up an online map to look at the roads near your current location to help your student pick a street. Once your student has selected a road, use online resources to find information about the particular road. Talk about how roads make it easier to get goods, have jobs, and access to other services.

Explore

Your student may struggle with comparing different types of transportation if they have not experienced some of the transportation options. For example, if you live in the suburbs and always have access to a car, your student may never know how difficult it is to walk to places for basic necessities such as buying groceries or doing laundry. Have a conversation about the different modes of transportation available. Ask probing questions such as, "How much longer and more difficult would it be to walk versus ride a bike?" You can use this model for having a discussion. Through discussion, show your student that transportation has evolved over time to make our lives easier.

Write (How did the Mediterranean Sea expand trade for the Romans?)

Your student may struggle to identify the specific impacts the Mediterranean Sea had on trade. Ask your student to summarize why the ancient Romans would want to travel by water, and then guide your student toward how water travel could help trade.

Learning Styles

Auditory learners may enjoy using navigation tools online and listening to the digital narration explain the route. This can be done through a search engine map service.

Visual learners may enjoy watching videos about the ways in which the ancient Romans traded. Your student can look up images of artifacts that show what the traded material looked like. They can also look at the ships that were used and some pictures of the roads.

Kinesthetic learners may enjoy tracing with their fingers the routes that Romans used to trade. This allows for your student to see the relative location of the trading partners and the distances they travelled in order to trade supplies.

Extension Activities

Research the Route

Have your student think about the path of the Silk Trade Road that Romans and other civilizations used for trade. What would the Romans need if they wanted to travel along this route? Have them talk to you about what the Romans would need to successfully travel this route.

Trade Brochure

Have your student select one of the goods that the Romans offered to other countries (i.e. olive oil, pottery, or papyrus). Have them create a brochure convincing people to trade things for this item. What would the Romans want in exchange for the item they have selected? Why would other countries want this item?

Answer Key

Write *(How did the Romans improve transportation?)*

Answers will vary. Possible answer: The Romans created roads to transport their goods. The roads facilitated travel from place to place and provided a lot of economic benefits from the import and transport of goods.

Write *(How did the Mediterranean Sea expand trade for the Romans?)*

Answers will vary. Possible answer: The Mediterranean Sea provided access for the transportation of large quantities of goods and allowed the Romans to reach places inaccessible to them by land.

Practice

Spain: metals

Africa: spices, silks, ivory

China: silks, spices, jewelry, finer materials for clothes

Show What You Know

1. D
2. A, B, D
3. B
4. Roman roads
5. Mediterranean Sea
6. Answers will vary. Possible answer: The Romans changed transportation by creating paved and convenient roads for the people to use for trading and travel.

Lesson Objectives

By the end of this lesson, your student will be able to:

- describe how the Pax Romana was important and how it affected the Roman Empire
- identify and describe the social classes of Ancient Rome before and after the Pax Romana

Supporting Your Student

Explore

For this section, your student is required to think of the pros and cons of two different types of societies. By doing so, they are activating their prior knowledge and engaging in critical thinking. You can help your student by describing a "perfect society" scenario. They can then analyze the pros and cons from that scenario. You can also help your student by describing a war society. What is it like for the citizens? How is it for the economy? How does conflict impact the citizens? Use guiding questions and scenarios to deepen thinking.

Read (A Golden Age)

It is important for your student to have a good understanding of the previous two lessons to get the most understanding out of the Pax Romana period. Help them remember important topics by asking guiding questions like, "How did constant warfare affect the Republic?," "How did bringing in so many enslaved people affect plebeians in Rome?," and "What did the generals do to increase division among Roman citizens?"

Practice

During this activity, your student is required to think about different aspects of Roman society and how they were impacted by Pax Romana. You can support your student through this activity by discussing each part of Roman society and asking your student to summarize the details. You can also assist your student by asking them guiding questions about how these elements changed during Pax Romana, such as "What was this part of society like before Pax Romana?" or "What was this part of society like after Pax Romana?"

Learning Styles

Auditory learners may enjoy discussing how they think peace can impact a society as they learn about the different impacts of Pax Romana on Rome.

Visual learners may enjoy watching videos about the advances of this time, whether it is about the economics, the social classes, the architecture, or another interest. Your student may also like to look at the transition in Rome's appearance from the time of war versus the time of peace. This could visualize for them how Rome's prosperity shifted over time.

Kinesthetic learners may enjoy drawing some of the buildings after researching them. Your student can also find images of the Pax Romana period and make a collage.

Extension Activities

Pax Romana Research

Augustus and Pax Romana gave way to artists, writers, entertainers, craftsmen, and much more. Since it was a time of peace, society became focused on the things that make life enjoyable, not just survivable. Have your student research the contributions that were made during this time to these topics. Have them write a paragraph explaining the contributions. Then have them draw a picture to show the contribution or print one from the computer.

A Life at Peace

Have your student consider this question: If your life was entirely at peace, what would you do? Remind them that like the Pax Romana, it does not necessarily mean a life free from fighting. But what would they be able to do with the time and resources available, without anything holding them back? Have them make a list of ideas and goals they could create if they had their own Pax Personalis. How would a time of peace help them accomplish their goals?

Answer Key

Explore

Answers will vary. Possible answers:

Pros of a Society at War: War could be positive for society because they could gain more land, create changes in their government, and gain new things that could help the society make money like new goods or materials from other lands.

Cons of a Society at War: War could be negative for society because it uses a lot of money and resources from the country and is very dangerous for the people.

Pros of a Society at Peace: Peace could be positive for society because it could allow the people to grow and make positive changes without being worried about conflict with other nations. The country could focus on improving parts of their own government, lives, or economy, which take time to improve.

Cons of a Society at Peace: Peace could be negative for a society because other countries could view them as weak or vulnerable.

Answers will vary. Possible answer: A society at peace is more desirable because it is safer and has more opportunity for improvement.

Write (What does Pax Romana mean? Was it truly a 200 year period of complete peace?)

Answers will vary. Possible answer: Pax Romana literally meant "Roman Peace" and was a period that was very prosperous for the Roman Empire. It wasn't a literal peace, as there were still conflicts.

Write (Identify three major advancements Rome invested in during Pax Romana.)

Answers will vary. Possible answers: trade, roads, engineering/aqueducts, building, discovering concrete

Practice

Answers will vary. Possible answers:

Economy: The Roman economy flourished during the Pax Romana as trade with other countries increased and more roads were built, making Rome even more powerful than before.

Social Classes: The strict line between social classes began to blur during the Pax Romana as each social class began to work with and support other social classes.

Art and Engineering: Art and engineering were given a space to grow during the Pax Romana. Creatives were given a chance to write and perform more of their works, and engineering accomplishments like the Pantheon and the Colosseum were built.

Show What You Know

1. C
2. False
3. Augustus
4. B
5. A
6. C

Lesson Objectives

By the end of this lesson, your student will be able to:

- identify key cultural contributions of ancient Roman civilization still around today
- describe the architectural characteristics of the Colosseum and the Pantheon

Supporting Your Student

Take a Closer Look

For this activity, your student is required to research a poet from ancient Rome. Have them start by reading poetry from each of the three poets. Ask your student which one they feel they connect with the most or is the most interesting to them. Use the internet to research that poet and learn information about their lives, their writing, and their contributions to ancient Rome. As your student finds this information, encourage them to take notes to help outline their paragraph.

Write *(What purpose did the Roman Colosseum serve in ancient times, and how does it connect to modern times?)*

Your student may struggle to answer both parts of this question on their first try. If your student is stuck, help them break the question down by guiding them to first think about what purpose the Colosseum had in ancient times, then think about how it connects to modern times.

Practice

Your student may struggle to find the similarities between the two buildings. Ask guiding questions, such as, "How were the buildings constructed? What do they both have in common? Why are they both continuously being discussed in ancient Roman history?" Your student can think about the materials used, the current condition of each building, and the architectural advances Rome made to secure both of the buildings for many years.

Learning Styles

Auditory learners may enjoy listening to readings from writers of this time, music from this time, and/or videos about advances during this period in Rome.

Visual learners may enjoy looking up pictures of the inside of ancient Roman buildings. Your student would benefit from seeing how the buildings look and the contributions they had to ancient Roman society, as well as why they are still important today.

Kinesthetic learners may enjoy creating a model or sketching a floor plan of an ancient Roman building such as the Colosseum or Pantheon. Encourage your student to clearly include elements of Roman architecture in their model or sketch.

Extension Activities

Virtual Tour

Have your student explore a virtual tour of the Colosseum online. Have them record what they see in a paragraph or write a story about their journey as if they were truly there.

Brochure

Have your student create a brochure for tourists who want to visit the Pantheon, outlining key features, why people should visit the Pantheon, and important historical facts and information.

Answer Key

Write *(What purpose did the Roman Colosseum have in ancient times, and how does it connect to modern times?)*

Answers will vary. Possible answer: The Roman Colosseum served as a stadium for entertainment in ancient times. Popular entertainment included gladiator fights, sea battles, and much more. The free entertainment boosted the emperor's popularity. In modern times many stadiums are designed similarly to the Colosseum so that spectators can see the action from all sides.

Practice

Answers will vary. Possible answers:

Colosseum—fits 50,000 spectators, used for entertainment, open all around, took eight years to build, built by slaves

Both—built using materials found or created, concrete, structural support so they wouldn't fall or collapse, lasted until modern times due to architectural features, bronze, bricks

Pantheon—best preserved Roman building, religious temple, dome, thick walls, three parts, home to all of the gods, different types of concrete throughout, oculus

Show What You Know

1. False
2. True
3. A, C, D, E
4. A
5. B
6. A
7. C

Lesson Objectives

By the end of this lesson, your student will be able to:

- describe the problems that arose from Rome's expansion
- trace the factors that led to the collapse of the Roman Empire

Supporting Your Student

Explore

Your student may have varying degrees of awareness about the area in which they live. Assist them by guiding any research they do on the geography of their area and comparing it to the size and geography of the Roman Empire. As your student considers potential threats, ask them about various landforms or physical features that could provide protection or increase danger.

Write (What do you think was the greatest issue facing the Roman Empire at this time?)

Your student may struggle to identify which issue they think was the most impactful on the fall of ancient Rome. To help your student make a decision, encourage them to summarize the effects of each issue. Once your student has thought about all of the events, ask them to rank the effects of each issue from most important to least important. This exercise should guide your student toward being able to select an event to use for the writing question.

Practice

Your student may struggle finding the cause of events and the impact that they had on Rome. Use guiding questions to help your student separate the information and fill out the graphic organizer. Ask, "How did this event become a problem for ancient Rome?" and "How did this event lead to the fall of ancient Rome?"

Learning Styles

Auditory learners may enjoy hearing historians recount the events through videos or reading the text aloud. Your student may also like to engage in discussion with you about how ancient Rome rose to power and to collapse.

Visual learners may enjoy viewing maps of ancient Rome at its largest point and comparing them to a modern map of this area. Your student may enjoy pointing out differences between these maps and having a discussion about what historic events led to the changes.

Kinesthetic learners may enjoy playing charades to act out the impacts of certain events of the Roman Empire. Your student may also benefit from creating flashcards that include key information about each contribution to the Roman Empire's demise.

Extension Activities

Creating a Solution

With all of the problems that arose, it is hard to imagine they didn't have solutions! In retrospect we can see that some of the problems could have been fixed or avoided, and that perhaps the Roman Empire could have faced a different result. For their task, have your student pick one or two of the problems that ancient Rome faced, as addressed in the lesson. Have them write a solution proposal that makes sense for the time period and would assist in alleviating the problem. The solution proposal should be one to two paragraphs outlining how Romans could fix the problem, possible solutions, and how this would impact the Roman Empire overall. In an additional paragraph, have your student explain their thinking and reasoning. Make sure they use evidence and their own knowledge to support their claims.

Creating a Timeline

Have your student research all of the issues that contributed to the fall of ancient Rome and put them on a timeline with dates. This will allow them to see the change over time and how each event contributed to ancient Rome's downfall.

Sunny, Scenic Ancient Rome!

Your student can synthesize their learning by creating a travel brochure about ancient Rome. Have them research a place from ancient times and use all the information to inform their audience about the location and to influence them to visit. Suggested inclusions to the brochure:

- Location: map, geography, major cities
- Important places: historic sites, and landmarks
- What you can do for fun activities, sports, water, entertainment
- Weather and Climate
- Transportation options
- Pictures

Answer Key

Write *(What do you think was the greatest issue facing the Roman Empire at this time?)*
Answers will vary. Possible answer: Poor leadership caused many issues for the ancient Roman Empire. There were many leaders in a short period of time, and the emperors often spent the money in foolish ways.

Practice
Answers will vary. Possible answers:

Event	Cause	Effect
Splitting the Empire	Emperor Diocletian tried to solve Rome's problems by splitting the empire in two, making it easier to govern.	This eventually weakened the empire even more. The Eastern and Western Roman empires began to drift apart as the Eastern empire grew stronger and the Western empire weaker.
Barbarians	The word *barbarian* comes from a Greek word for "babbler". That was what the Greeks called anyone who was not a Greek and did not speak their language. The Romans adopted the word and used it for those who lived outside the Roman Empire.	They all wanted Roman lands, and eventually they were able to overrun the Western empire and bring it to an end. In 476 AD, a man named Odoacer from one of the barbarian tribes removed Emperor Romulus Augustulus from his throne in Rome, and that was the end of the Western Empire.
Poor Leadership	Emperor Marcus Aurelius' death in 180 AD. He was the last of the strong and effective emperors.	Rome entered a time of confusion and instability, when military leaders battled each other for power. Most emperors of this period lasted only a short time in power.
Slave Labor	The Roman Legions brought home captives as slaves whenever they conquered a new territory. The slaves worked in the fields and crafted the tools and household items that Romans needed.	When the empire stopped expanding, there were no new slaves arriving and, therefore, not enough workers to keep the economy going.
Money Problems	The expanding empire brought in wealth and slaves from the conquered areas. Eventually Rome ran out of areas to conquer.	Many of the Roman emperors were foolish in their use of money and built grand palaces for themselves rather than using the funds to govern the people and build the empire.
Weakening of the Army	Many Romans didn't want to serve in the army anymore because it meant long months away from their families, and the pay was not good.	The empire had to hire outsiders to serve in its army. These foreigners did not have the same commitment to Rome as did the former Legions, and their independent attitudes broke down the army's discipline.

Show What You Know
1. False

2. C

3. B

4. D

5. A

6. Answers will vary. Possible answer: Splitting the empire caused each side of the empire to become disconnected, which led to the Western Roman Empire falling apart.

Lesson Objectives

By the end of this lesson, your student will review the following big ideas from Chapter 8.

- Italy has significant geographical features such as being a boot-shaped peninsula, having many mountain ranges, and sharing borders with France and Switzerland. (Lesson 48)
- The Roman Republic created a code of written laws called the Law of the Twelve Tables to make life more balanced between the different social classes. (Lesson 49)
- Ancient Rome successfully conquered many people and lands, eventually integrating some of these cultures and their customs into their way of life. (Lesson 50)
- The Roman Empire built a highly advanced road system, developed trade relationships throughout the ancient world, and created extensive trade routes that reached as far as Britain and possibly parts of Asia. (Lesson 51)
- The Pax Romana, or "Roman peace," improved the quality of life for all classes. (Lesson 52)
- Ancient Roman civilization made many key cultural contributions that are still around today, including concrete. (Lesson 53)
- Many problems arose from Rome's expansion and contributed to the collapse of the Roman Empire. (Lesson 54)

Supporting Your Student

Practice (Three's a Crowd)
Your student may struggle to draw connections between the words in each group. To help your student identify the connection and which word does not fit in the group, ask them to define each word, then ask them if they feel any of the words are similar or stick out from the others. Repeat this process any time your student feels stuck on one of the questions.

Practice (Tracking Changes)
Your student may struggle to identify specific changes in each aspect of Roman life. To help your student identify changes, ask them to summarize each aspect of life in different times in Rome—from the days of Roman kings, to the Republic, to the Empire, to the fall of the Empire. As the student summarizes life in the different time periods, they should be able to identify differences and changes that occurred over time.

Practice (Decide the Difference)
Your student may feel overwhelmed with trying to identify similarities and differences between the Roman Republic and the Roman Empire. Encourage your student to analyze the two types of government one at a time. They should list as much information as they can regarding that type of government before switching to the other type of government. Once your student has listed information about each type of government, encourage them to identify similarities and differences between the two lists that they can record on the Venn diagram.

Learning Styles

Auditory learners may enjoy discussing differences between the Roman Republic and Roman Empire before recording these ideas on the Venn diagram.

Visual learners may enjoy reviewing different maps of the Roman Republic, Roman Empire, and modern-day Italy to see how the area has changed over time. Consider researching different maps of the area with your student.

Kinesthetic learners may enjoy creating and using flashcards with different information they learned about Rome.

Extension Activities

Creating a Timeline
Have your student create a timeline with at least two important events from each lesson in the chapter. These events should span from the genesis of Rome to its downfall. Once the timeline is created, review it with your student.

Poster Presentation

Have your student create a poster containing information about life in ancient Rome. Ask them to include images of art and architecture, details about the government, and information about what life was like in ancient Rome. After they have created their poster, have them present the information to you as though they are teaching you about ancient Rome.

Answer Key

Write (How did life change for plebeians between the Period of Kings and the Republic?)

Answers will vary. Possible answers: plebeians got more political power, assemblies were created so plebeians had a voice in government, laws were written down so everyone would know them, laws were applied more equally

Practice (Three's a Crowd)

1. senate; It is not a building created by the Romans.
2. aqueduct; It is not a type of government the Romans experienced.
3. kings; They were not a class on the social hierarchy.
4. Pax Romana; It does not have anything to do with trading goods.
5. Triumvirate; It did not relate to Roman religion.

Practice (Tracking Changes)

Part of Roman Life	Changes Over Time
Government	Rome was ruled by kings at first, then it became a republic so the people could be involved in the decisions, and then it was an empire with one emperor making all the choices.
Social Class	The social classes were very structured at first, but during Pax Romana they became more flexible.
Architecture	Over time the Romans created many monumental structures such as roads, the Pantheon, and the Colosseum.
Military	The strong Roman military which helped them grow, but eventually it grew weak and contributed to their downfall.

Practice (Decide the Difference)

Answers will vary. Possible answers:

Republic: ruled by consuls, senate, and assemblies

Empire: had one emperor

Both: military was important, trade was important, religion was important

Quick Review

Refer to the statement your student circled in the Show What You Know section to self-assess their knowledge of the chapter concepts. Then to assist in determining if your student is ready to take the assessment, consider:

- Having your student summarize the strengths of the Roman Republic and the strengths of the Roman Empire.
- Having your student name parts of Rome.

Discover! SOCIAL STUDIES • GRADE 6 • CHAPTER 8 ASSESSMENT

165

Chapter Assessment

Circle the correct answer for each question.

1. Which of the following statements are true about Italy? Circle all correct answers.

   A. It includes mountains.

   B. It is entirely surrounded by water.

   C. It has water on three sides.

   D. It borders other countries including France, Austria, and Switzerland.

2. How did Pax Romana impact Rome? Circle all correct answers.

   A. The Romans created new art and architecture.

   B. The Romans won many wars.

   C. The Romans made the social hierarchy more flexible.

   D. The Romans created a new form of government.

3. The Romans changed transportation by creating _____.

   A. the wheel

   B. roads

   C. carts

   D. ways to ride animals

4. What was the main trade route created by the Romans?

   A. the Pantheon

   B. the Colosseum

   C. the Silk Road

   D. the Mediterranean Sea

5. True or False   The etruscans were the earliest settlers in Italy.

6. True or False   Rome changed from a republic to an empire after the Triumvirate failed and Octavian took over as the sole ruler of Rome.

7. True or False   The weakened military, poor leadership, money problems, barbarians, and splitting of the empire all led to the fall of the Roman Empire.

Match each type of Roman government to its description.

8. _____ republic

9. _____ empire

10. _____ triumvirate

   A. a government with three leaders who all work together

   B. a government where the people elect representatives to help make decisions

   C. a government where one leader makes all of the decisions

Match each Roman creation to what it was used for.

11. ____ roads

12. ____ Pantheon

13. ____ Colosseum

14. ____ Law of Twelve Tables

    A. to honor the gods and hold religious services

    B. to make transportation easier

    C. to allow people to watch events

    D. to explain the rights of the Roman citizens

15. Put the social hierarchy of Ancient Rome in order from 1 (highest) to 5 (lowest).

    ____ equites

    ____ freedmen

    ____ patricians

    ____ slaves

    ____ plebeians

Answer the following questions in complete sentences.

16. Describe the branches of the Roman Republic and their purpose.

....

....

....

....

....

....

....

17. How did religion in Rome change over time?

....

....

....

....

....

....

....

....

Chapter Assessment Answer Key

1. A, C, D

2. A, C

3. B

4. C

5. True

6. True

7. True

8. B

9. C

10. A

11. B

12. A

13. C

14. D

15. 2, 4, 1, 5, 3

16. Answers will vary. Possible answer: The Roman Republic had two consuls that formed the highest part of the government and controlled the military, a senate made up of patricians who advised the consuls, and assemblies made up of patricians and plebeians, who worked together to create laws.

17. Answers will vary. Possible answer: The Roman religion was first inspired by the Greeks, so they worshipped many gods, but the Romans eventually converted to Christianity.

Alternative Assessment

Project: Podcast

Your student may create and present a podcast about ancient Rome. It should include information about the Roman hierarchy, Roman trade with the rest of the world, the Pax Romana, and the factors that led to the collapse of the Roman Empire. Your student may present their podcast to their friends and their instructor or just their instructor.

Project Requirements or Steps:

1. Brainstorm all of the parts of your podcast:

   A. Roman hierarchy

   B. Roman trade with the rest of the world

   C. The Pax Romana

   D. Factors that led to the collapse of the Roman Empire

2. Organize the information for your podcast.

3. Write your podcast script.

4. Practice your podcast.

5. Record and present your podcast to your friends and instructor.

Discover! SOCIAL STUDIES • GRADE 6 • CHAPTER 8 ASSESSMENT

169

Alternative Assessment Rubric

Use the following rubric to grade your student's assessment.

	4	3	2	1	Points
Connection to the Chapter	The podcast includes all components and is connected to the chapter.	The podcast includes most components and is somewhat connected to the chapter.	The podcast includes some components and is somewhat connected to the chapter.	The podcast does not include any components and is not connected to the chapter.	
Creativity	The podcast is very creative and original.	The podcast is creative.	The podcast is somewhat creative.	The podcast is not creative.	
Organization	The podcast is organized and reads smoothly.	The podcast is mostly organized and reads somewhat smoothly.	The podcast is somewhat organized, but it does not read smoothly.	The podcast is somewhat organized, but it does not read smoothly.	
Grammar and Mechanics	The speech is clear and grammatically correct.	The speech is mostly clear with one or two grammar errors.	The speech is somewhat clear with several grammar errors.	The speech has a distracting number of grammar errors.	

Total Points _____/16

Average _____

Lesson Objectives

By the end of this lesson, your student will be able to:

- locate on a map the site of the ancient Mesoamerican civilizations
- analyze the obstacles to discovering the origins and history of ancient Mesoamerican civilizations

Supporting Your Student

Explore

There are great resources online that give greater detail about the Choctaw Tribe. Have your student search and read about the Choctaw origin stories. Many websites dedicated to this history include pictures as well. Encourage your student to think about each story by asking them which of the stories is more believable or if being believable makes a story true. Help them look for truth in both stories.

Read *(Mesoamerica)*

If you have a globe, encourage your student to find where ancient Mesoamerica is. Help them identify where in the world it is, and talk about the people that are known to live in that region. Explain how those people are Indigenous.

Learning Styles

Auditory learners may enjoy listening to videos on YouTube about Mesoamerican civilizations.

Visual learners may enjoy creating their own masks to look like those of the Olmec culture. There are a lot of great resources online for creating masks that look like the Olmec-style mask.

Kinesthetic learners may enjoy turning themselves into a human sundial. Have your student take a picture of themselves from the knees down in a specific spot outside, when sunny. A few hours later, have them return to the spot and take the same picture. The student should be sure to capture their shadow and the direction it is facing. Ask them to determine by their shadow what time of day it is.

Extension Activities

Virtual Field Trip

Many great resources can be found online. The Arizona Museum of Natural History has an extensive listing online that shows many artifacts from ancient Mesoamerica. One that is very well-known is the Faces of Mesoamerica artifact. They also display several pictures of the pyramids located in the area. Another great resource is found on Chichén Itzá's website. There you can see what it looks like in a video! There are other great resources to discover the history of the Ancient Mesoamerican Civilizations!

Ancient Mesoamerican Civilizations

Answer Key

Write *(What kind of written language did Mesoamerican cultures have?)*

Mesoamerican cultures wrote with hieroglyphs, like the Cascajal Block.

Write *(What other stories have you heard that are similar to the verbal history of the Choctaw? What do you think likely happened?)*

Answers will vary. Your student's answer should include critical thinking answers, such as "If I were going to cross the ocean, I might have done it on a raft."

Show What You Know

1. B
2. B
3. A
4. C
5. god

Ancient Olmec Civilization

Lesson Objectives

By the end of this lesson, your student will be able to:

- analyze the possible migrations of people to the continents of North and South America
- describe key historical events of the Olmec civilization
- identify how the Olmecs impacted or influenced other Mesoamerican civilizations

Supporting Your Student

In the Real World

You can guide your student in their research by suggesting search queries like "discovery of rubber" or "Olmecs using latex from rubber tree" if they need support finding good information. Your student may also enjoy watching videos of traditional latex harvesting.

Read (Where Did the Olmecs Come From?)

Activate your student's prior knowledge by asking guiding questions before they read. You can ask, "What have you learned about Mesoamerica so far?," "Where is Mesoamerica located?," and "How do you think the environment of this area has had an impact on human settlement?"

Read (Influence and Legacy of Olmec Culture)

Previewing and predicting are important reading strategies to increase retention and comprehension. Ask your student to preview this section by scanning, then predicting the ways Olmec culture influenced others. You can ask additional guiding questions based on their prediction, such as "How did other ancient cultures influence others?" and "How do cultures influence each other?"

Learning Styles

Auditory learners may enjoy listening to aerophone and ocarina music from Mesoamerica.

Visual learners may enjoy labeling a map of Mesoamerica with important details about Olmec civilization.

Kinesthetic learners may enjoy trying to play hip-ulama, the contemporary version of the Mesoamerican ball game.

Extension Activities

Compare and Contrast: Tree Tapping

Rubber is not the only thing extracted from trees! In fact, sugar can be extracted from trees as well. Have your student research traditional latex harvesting and maple syrup harvesting. They can complete a Venn diagram on the similarities and differences of harvesting and processing both products for use.

Virtual Field Trip

Your student can go on a virtual tour of the archeological park at La Venta (also known as the parque-museo). To extend their learning after viewing the virtual tour, ask them to write a short essay on the importance of preserving historical sites such as this one.

Answer Key

Write *(How did the environment and geography of the area influence the Olmec civilization?)*
Answers will vary. Possible answer: The environment was very important to the Olmecs because they based their society around the river networks, using them for agriculture, transportation, and trade.

Practice
Answers will vary. Possible answer: emergence of Olmec civilization in 1500 BC, decline and destruction of San Lorenzo Tenochtitlán in 900 BC, shifting central hub of civilization to La Venta around 900 BC, environmental changes of 900 BC, emergence of Olmec influences on society in Zazacatla around 800 BC, decline of Olmec civilization around 400 BC.

Write *(In what ways did the Olmec civilization influence others who came later?)*
Answers will vary. Possible answer: hierarchical society, trade (especially of luxury items), religious practices, agriculture, carvings, art, the Mesoamerican ballgame, uses for rubber

Show What You Know
1. The <u>Olmec</u> are considered Mesoamerica's first <u>civilization</u>, emerging from the farming cultures around Tabasco, <u>Mexico</u>. They lived across the gulf lowlands of present-day Tabasco and <u>Veracruz</u>. The center of their civilization began as San Lorenzo Tenochtitlán. The Olmec civilization thrived from roughly 1500 BC to 400 BC. The Olmec originated in the <u>Americas</u>, based on DNA evidence of ancient Olmec remains.

2. False
3. True
4. True
5. False
6. True
7. False
8. True

Ancient Mayan Civilization

Lesson Objectives

By the end of this lesson, your student will be able to:

- trace the history of the Maya as they developed into a civilization
- evaluate the contribution of Diego de Landa to the knowledge of the Maya
- identify the government structure of Mayan civilization and how we learned about it

Supporting Your Student

Explore

To assist your student, help them understand that history can never be pinned down to an exact truth. Both the people that wrote history and those who read it each have a unique perspective. Scientific experiments are true because repeating an experiment exactly will yield the same results. History cannot be repeated, only explained.

In the Real World

If your student is unfamiliar with what a UNESCO World Heritage Site is, explain that they are landmarks throughout the world that have significant cultural, historical, or scientific importance. They are protected by the United Nations Educational Scientific and Cultural Organization.

Read *(Cracking the Code)*

Your student may need help understanding that for a period of about 350 years from 1478 to 1834, the Catholic Church enacted a specific set of laws generally known as the Spanish Inquisition. The official duty of the Inquisition was to force non-Christians to convert to Christianity. Anyone who did not convert could be killed. De Lande had to answer to the Inquisition and this explains how he had the power to order Mayan books destroyed.

Learning Styles

Auditory learners may enjoy listening to native speakers of Mayan languages.

Visual learners may enjoy viewing Mayan artworks.

Kinesthetic learners may enjoy building models of Mayan temples.

Extension Activities

Visit Chichen Itza!

Your student can explore Chichen Itza through a virtual field trip to see what it looked like and what important historical artifacts or ruins can be found there.

Mayans Today

There are millions of descendants of Mayan culture living in Mesoamerica today. Your student can research how they are keeping their culture alive and create a poster displaying their research.

Answer Key

Write *(Why did Mayan influence diminish after 950 CE?)*

Answers will vary. Possible answer: We only have theories, not facts. Theories include war, over-farming poor soils, and drought.

Practice

Answers will vary. Possible answer:

Preclassic: sedentary communities, cultivating crops, cities and villages, inscribed monuments, pyramid building, Mayan script developed

Classic: villages and cities developed into powerful city-states, trade and culture allowed for the development of a kind of middle class

Postclassic: warfare, disease, environmental disasters, people began to move out of city-states that collapsed and moved northward, European colonizers began to arrive

Show What You Know

1. Preclassic, Classic, Postclassic

2. Preclassic

3. Classic

4. Postclassic

5. Preclassic

6. Postclassic

7. Answers will vary. Possible answer: Kings did not have absolute power. They were responsible to the opinions and desires of their sponsors.

8. Answers will vary. Possible answer: Diego de Landa did record a lot of information about Mayan culture in his book, but he also destroyed primary sources. The destruction made it harder for later historians.

Lesson Objectives

By the end of this lesson, your student will be able to:

- discuss the different elements of the economy of the Mayan civilization
- sequence the steps of Mayan farming during the dry season
- describe why cacao beans were important to the Mayan civilization

Supporting Your Student

Explore

Remind your student that what a culture trades is often based on the available resources. Ask your student what they remember about Olmec agriculture and economy before reading to activate prior knowledge. Ask your student if they think there will be any similarities between Mayan and Olmec trade and agriculture.

In the Real World *(Trading Goods)*

Begin considering what you might offer in exchange for certain items while your student makes their list. Try to create exchange values that are realistic and would best mirror a real-world exchange.

Take a Closer Look *(Basic and Luxury)*

Our view of what constitutes luxury today is not exactly the same as the ancient Mayans, but reinforcing that basic items are useful and/or relied on in daily life should help your student understand the distinction.

Learning Styles

Auditory learners may enjoy listening to a podcast about gardening techniques to learn more about the logic behind different planting methods.

Visual learners may enjoy creating their own map of Mayan trade routes.

Kinesthetic learners may enjoy making a dish using staple Mayan crops.

Extension Activities

Garden like a Mayan

Your student can build a simple raised bed (with supervision, especially if using power tools). Look for basic raised bed plans online for your student to follow, and assist as needed. When completed, plant seasonal produce and observe the growing process.

Swap Meet

Your student can organize a toy or clothing swap with their friends. They can gather all the items they would like to trade and meet to exchange items. After the swap, they should consider how the trading process went, if it was difficult to agree on exchange values, and if the participants left satisfied with their trades.

Answer Key

Write *(Write three examples of each type of item the Mayans traded.)*

Answers will vary. Possible answer:

Basic: clothing, basic furniture and ceramics, household goods, produce, tools

Luxury: fine textiles; fine furniture; fine ceramics; metal ornaments or sculptures; carved stone ornaments or sculptures; things made of gold, jade, obsidian, copper, or bronze

Show What You Know

1. False
2. True
3. True
4. False
5. False
6. True
7. False
8. B
9. C
10. A
11. Circled: farming techniques, large network of trade routes, produced many types of items

Lesson Objectives

By the end of this lesson, your student be able to:

- distinguish social class characteristics of the Maya
- analyze the Mayan religion
- describe the daily lives of the levels in Mayan society
- describe Mayan achievements

Supporting Your Student

Explore

You can support your student by helping them understand that humans have sought to explain the mysteries of life in many ways. Because the movement of the stars and constellations corresponds with the seasons, some cultures developed religions that explained the mysteries through astrology. You may also help your student to understand that astronomy is the science that studies the properties and structure of everything outside of the earth's atmosphere. Astrology is a pseudo-science that uses math to predict the effect of the heavens on human events.

Read *(Mayan Social Classes)*

Your student may struggle to understand the idea of hereditary class systems because those systems are inherently unfair. If this happens, reassure your student that they are understanding the point of studying history. History often teaches us mistakes to avoid.

Read *(Mayan Religion)*

Your student may be horrified by the idea of human sacrifice. This may provide you with the opportunity for home religious instruction by comparing Mayan beliefs to your own faith.

Learning Styles

Auditory learners may enjoy documentary features about Mayan culture or Mayan archeology.

Visual learners may enjoy exploring three-dimensional models of Mayan pyramids or ruins on the internet.

Kinesthetic learners may enjoy building their own Mayan pyramid from household items.

Extension Activities

Chichen Itza Travel Log

Have your student research all the things to do at the Chichen Itza historical park in Mexico. Have them create a three-day travel log about a visit to the site during the fall equinox.

Archeologist

Have your student learn the name of a famous Mesoamerican archeologist and make a short report about the archaeologist's training and discoveries.

Answer Key

Write *(Mayan social structure stressed the divine nature of the noble class. Does this system exist in the modern world?)*
Answers will vary. Possible answers: No, there is no noble class in a modern democracy. Yes, some countries still follow social systems and have nobility, even if not clearly defined.

Write *(Why do you think there were stories about the corn god fighting death?)*
Answers should focus on the idea that food (corn) provides life and that life is the enemy of death.

Practice
All answers should be yes.

Show What You Know
1. astrology
2. nobility
3. corn god
4. pyramids
5. calendar
6. C
7. A
8. C
9. A
10. D

Lesson Objectives

By the end of this lesson, your student will be able to:

• describe the decline of the Mayan civilization
• trace the migration and development of the Aztec civilization
• evaluate the economy of the Aztec civilization
• compare and contrast the Aztec and the Maya

Supporting Your Student

Explore

You can help your student to understand that origin myths often dress up the facts. This section is much less exciting than the myth that the Mexica left their home because a god told them to do so. Historians look for grains of truth in origin myths to try to create a realistic explanation.

Read (Decline of the Maya)

Help your student understand that historians look for patterns. Although we do not know exactly what happened to the Maya, historians can hypothesize based on similar patterns. Some hypotheses can be tested against the evidence in the fossil record or by the effects that weather patterns leave in tree rings or soil layers.

Read (Tribute and Empire)

To help your student understand this section, consider drawing a comparison to the fall of Rome from the invaders' points of view. At some point prior to 1200 AD, the population of the Valley of Mexico rapidly declined. The Toltecs filled the gap first then the Chichimec tribes followed. Like the Goths did in Rome, the Chichimec invaders adopted the trappings of the Toltec culture.

Learning Styles

Auditory learners may enjoy listening to short study guides on the Maya and Aztec available on the internet.

Visual learners may enjoy a virtual museum visit to an exhibit on the Aztec.

Kinesthetic learners may enjoy acting out the Explore vignette with added details of their own.

Extension Activities

Quetzalcoatl

Have your student prepare a slideshow about the Mesoamerican deity the Aztecs called Quetzalcoatl. Have them present the information to your instructor.

Dendrochronology

Have your student prepare a two to three minute oral report on dendrochronology, the science of studying tree rings to map the weather. This is a science used by many archaeologists when determining the reasons why civilizations disappeared or migrated.

Answer Key

Write *(What were the three foundations of the Aztec economy?)*

agriculture, trade, and tribute

Practice

Maya: few social classes, slash and burn agriculture

Aztec: many social classes, sustainable agriculture, demanded tribute, long-distance trade

Both: calendar, cacao currency

Show What You Know

1. True
2. False
3. False
4. True
5. True
6. False
7. False
8. False
9. True
10. True
11. Answers will vary. Possible answer: The people who spoke related languages were probably related. Mapping where similar languages were spoken may show how the language spread from an original homeland.

Lesson Objectives

By the end of this lesson, your student will be able to:

- describe the Aztec social structure
- analyze Aztec beliefs
- discuss the significance of the Aztec language and technological advances

Supporting Your Student

Read *(Aztec Advances)*

Explain to your student that the Nahuatl language still is used in small communities in central Mexico. Draw a generalization to all Native American languages. All these languages are dwindling, and most are in danger of being lost completely. Colonial languages such as Spanish and English have replaced most native languages. Make students aware of steps being taken to preserve the languages, such as creating recordings of native speakers and taking classes in school.

Read *(Aztec Social Order)*

This section contains disturbing content about human sacrifice. Make sure to prepare your student by warning that some of the content may be sad and shocking as they read. Discuss the section with your student to help them process the content at their level of maturity.

Write *(Discuss the ways the Aztec civilization was both violent and innovative.)*

Help your student create a strong paragraph with a claim or thesis statement followed by text evidence. Explain to your student that writing prompts such as these allow for opinion, but encourage them to support their claim with evidence from the text.

Learning Styles

Auditory learners may enjoy recording a podcast about Aztec society.

Visual learners may enjoy watching videos and seeing images of the achievements and vibrant arts of the Aztec.

Kinesthetic learners may enjoy drawing a picture or making a model of the city of Tenochtitlán.

Extension Activities

Aztec Animals

Have your student research three animals sacred to the Aztecs—the quetzal, the jaguar, and the monarch butterfly. Have them learn about the animal and their role in Aztec beliefs.

An Aztec Kid

Have your student dive deeper into daily life in the Aztec Empire. Have them use two or more credible online sources to learn about the daily life of a child in the Aztec Empire. Have them create a poster, brochure, or slide show to explain the findings. Key components should include daily routine, family, school, clothes, food, and games.

Answer Key

Write *(How did the Aztecs change the land of the central Mexican Valley to meet their needs?)*

Answers will vary. Possible answers: Causeways and bridges were built for people to travel. Floating gardens were built. A system of dikes and aqueducts controlled the water.

Write *(Discuss the ways the Aztec civilization was both violent and innovative.)*

Answers will vary. Possible answers: Aztec were brutal because they conquered others and performed sacrifices. Aztec were amazing because they had great arts and engineering. Both because they had great achievements but also performed brutal sacrifices.

Practice
Answers will vary. Possible answers:

Category	Accomplishment
architecture	designed temples, cities, bridges, canals, and floating gardens
art	created intricate, colorful designs on clothing, cloths, and paintings
communication	created a language, writing system, and mathematics
government	conquered a large empire

Show What You Know
1. C
2. A
3. B
4. False
5. False
6. True
7. False
8. True
9. Answers will vary. Possible answers: The highest class is the king, nobles, and high priests. Merchants, warriors, and craftsmen are a high class. Commoners and slaves worked in farming, fishing, and hunting.

Lesson Objectives

By the end of this lesson, your student will be able to:

- identify key landmarks on a map of Mesoamerica
- analyze the effect the Spanish conquest of Mexico had on the demise of the Maya and Aztec civilizations

Supporting Your Student

Read (Conquest of Mexico)

Explain to your student that Cortes arrived at a year that coincided with an Aztec prophecy. In this year, the god Quetzalcoatl was supposed to return to Earth and visit the Aztecs. When the Aztecs saw Cortes and his men, they did not look like any people they had ever seen. They also had no knowledge of horses. Their sight looked amazing and unbelievable to the Aztecs. The Aztecs thought Cortes may be Quetzalcoatl himself. This gave Cortes a strategic advantage.

Read (Legacy of the Conquest)

Discuss the immense transfer of goods, people, crops, and animals that occurred across the Atlantic after the colonization by Spain. Your student may be surprised to learn that typical farm animals such as chickens, cows, horses, and pigs were unknown in the Americas. Likewise, Europeans had never had chocolate or potatoes before the exchange. Though the exchange of goods and animals had some advantages, there were also exchanges of diseases. The Native Americans had lived in isolation for so long that they had no natural immunity and most died after contact with Europeans.

Explain the concept of genocide. Genocide differs from other forms of war because it is the extermination of nearly an entire people and their way of life. A very large percentage of native people of the Americas died due to the invasion by Europeans.

Learning Styles

Auditory learners may enjoy delivering a simulated first-person account from the point of view of an Aztec and a Spanish explorer.

Visual learners may enjoy using videos, images, and maps to support their understanding of the text.

Kinesthetic learners may enjoy creating their own map of Mexico and moving toy soldiers across the map to trace the Spanish route through Mexico.

Extension Activities

Comparison: Fall of the Incas

Have your student research the conquest of the Inca Empire by the Conquistador Francisco Pizarro. Have them make a list of similarities and differences to the conquest of the Aztecs by Cortes. Then using a comparison chart, Venn diagram, or another graphic organizer, have your student show the results.

Spanish Exploration

Have your student complete additional research about the voyages of exploration and invasion by other Spanish explorers and plot their mission locations on a map. Suggested explorers include:

- Columbus
- Balboa
- De Soto
- Pizarro
- De Vaca
- Ponce De Leon

Answer Key

Write *(Describe the motivations of the Spanish to conquer Mexico.)*

Answers will vary. Possible answers: to acquire gold and riches, to spread Christianity, to make Spain large and powerful

Practice

1. conquistador
2. Cortes
3. Christianity
4. Montezuma
5. genocide

Show What You Know

1. False
2. True
3. False
4. False
5. True
6. D
7. B
8. A
9. D
10. C

Lesson Objectives

By the end of this lesson, your student will review the following big ideas from Chapter 9.

- Powerful empires developed in Mesoamerica. The Olmecs built the first Mesoamerican empire based on trade. (Lesson 57)
- The religious beliefs of the Mayans and Aztecs influenced their society. (Lesson 58)
- The Mayans built a thriving economy based on trade of basic and luxury goods. (Lesson 59)
- The Mayans and Aztecs used a strict social structure. (Lesson 60)
- The Aztec economy was built on agriculture, trade, and tribute. (Lesson 61)
- The Aztecs made advancements in language and technology. (Lesson 62)
- The Spanish invaded and conquered Mesoamerica. (Lesson 63)

Supporting Your Student

Write (Why do you think so many powerful empires developed in this region?)

Explain that this question requires that your student make a theory grounded in the information learned. However, there is no one correct answer to find and repeat. Your student must use thinking skills to make an assertion. Ask your student why they think this and what information led to their conclusion.

Review (Rise and Fall of the Aztecs)

When your student studies the conquest of the Aztecs by the Spanish, ask them to consider multiple viewpoints. The Spanish, Aztecs, and neighboring tribes all interpreted the events very differently. Use this opportunity to explain that various groups of people often think of events differently because of how they were impacted, their cultural or religious beliefs, or their point of view. In this case, the conquistadors may have seen events as a great victory, while the Aztecs saw events as a terrible invasion.

Practice (Mesoamerican Empire Comparison Chart)

There are many similarities between the Mayans and the Aztecs. Make sure your student can determine differences and record them in the comparison chart. For example, the empires had different locations and farming techniques.

Learning Styles

Auditory learners may enjoy recording their own summary of the chapter content and listening to the recording for reinforcement.

Visual learners may enjoy viewing videos and images that represent the vocabulary used by these societies.

Kinesthetic learners may enjoy creating models or acting out scenes from the chapter.

Extension Activities

Museum Virtual Tour

Have your student complete an online search for museums in Mexico. Have them search terms such as "Mexico museum Aztec" or "Mexico museum Maya" to produce good results to start with. Have them view the galleries and artifacts at selected museums.

View the Region

Have your student use a satellite-based tool, such as Google Earth, to view Mesoamerica. Your student can study the Yucatan area and the central valley of Mexico. Some areas of interest may include Chichen Itza, Tulum, Teotenago, Teotihuacan, and Mexico City.

Answer Key

Write *(Why do you think so many powerful empires developed in this region?)*

Answers will vary. Possible answer: There were large supplies of gold and other resources. The people there developed great building skills.

Practice *(Visualizing Vocabulary)*

Drawings and sentences will vary. Your student's answer should demonstrate an understanding of vocabulary and concepts from the chapter.

Practice *(Mesoamerican Comparison Chart)*

Answers will vary. Possible answer: Mayan Empire: Yucatan, slash and burn, pyramids

Aztec Empire: Valle of Mexico, floating gardens, religious sacrifice

Practice *(Cause and Effect)*

1. A
2. F
3. D
4. C
5. E
6. B

Quick Review

Refer to the statement your student circled in the Show What You Know section to self-assess their knowledge of the chapter concepts. Then to assist in determining if your student is ready to take the assessment, consider:

- Having your student name the major Mesoamerican empire and their locations.
- Having your student describe the Mayan and Aztec social structures.
- Having your student describe how Hernan Cortes was able to defeat the Aztec Empire.

Discover! SOCIAL STUDIES • GRADE 6 • CHAPTER 9 ASSESSMENT

189

Chapter Assessment

Circle the correct answer.

1. True or False   The Olmec left behind enormous sculptures of heads.

2. True or False   Aztec civilization was made of many unique cultures that lived in present-day southern Mexico, Guatemala, Honduras, and Belize.

3. True or False   The Mayan civilization is divided into three periods: preclassic, classic, and postclassic.

4. True or False   The Olmec and Mayans also used "slash-and-burn" to clear forested areas for farming.

5. True or False   The Aztecs were warlike, so they were not artistic.

6. Which image was a common motif in Olmec art?

   A. Saltwater crocodile   **C.** flowers

   B. Were-jaguar

7. What are Mayan builders best known for?

   A. Prolific building of pyramids   **C.** Roadways that connected the empire

   B. Making floating gardens

8. Who was at the top of the Aztec social order?

   A. Farmers   **C.** Priests

   B. Craftspeople

9. Why did the Aztec practice ritual sacrifice?

   A. To show power in battle   **C.** To scare off Christian priests

   B. As an offering to the sun god

10. Why did the Spanish explore and conquer Mesoamerica? Circle all correct answers.

   A. To gain power for the ruler of Spain

   B. To find gold

   C. To convert native people to Christianity

Chapter Assessment Answer Key

1. True
2. False
3. True
4. True
5. False
6. B
7. A
8. C
9. B
10. A, B, C

Alternative Assessment

Project: Newspaper Article

A newspaper article is a piece of writing that covers the basic details of a recent or current news event by answering who, what, where, when, why, and how.

Project Requirements:

For this project, write a newspaper article about a topic that was covered in the chapter. This may be an actual historical event, such as "Cortes Enters Tenochtitlan" or a nonspecific event that may require imaging details, such as "Olmec Artists Makes Giant Stone Sculpture." You will research and convey information in an appealing, informative, and succinct manner.

Include the following elements in the newspaper article.

- Title
- Name
- Lead sentence or attention grabber
- Details of event or topic
- Summary ending
- List of interviewee and sources

Alternative Assessment Rubric

Use the following rubric to grade your student's assessment.

	4	3	2	1	Points
Relevant Content	The newspaper article makes clear and repetitive connections to the chapter and includes all the required elements.	The newspaper article makes one or two references to the chapter, but does not include all required elements.	The newspaper article is related to the chapter, but does not include all required elements.	The newspaper article is unrelated to the chapter and does not include the required elements	
Creativity	The newspaper article is very creative and aesthetically appealing.	The newspaper article is creative and aesthetically appealing.	The newspaper article is somewhat creative and aesthetically appealing.	The newspaper article is not creative or aesthetically appealing.	
Informative Content	The newspaper article is informative and conveys an event or topic from the chapter.	The newspaper article is somewhat informative and conveys an event or topic from the chapter.	The newspaper article is somewhat informative, but does not convey an event from the chapter.	The newspaper article is not informative and does not convey an event or topic from the chapter.	
Grammar and Mechanics	There are no grammar or punctuation mistakes.	There are one or two grammar or punctuation mistakes.	There are several grammar or punctuation mistakes.	There are a distracting number of grammar and punctuation mistakes.	

Total Points _____/16

Average _____

Discover! SOCIAL STUDIES • GRADE 6 • CHAPTER 9 ASSESSMENT

193

Lesson Objectives

By the end of this lesson, your student will be able to:

- locate Africa's major regions and ancient kingdoms on a map
- describe various geographic features of Africa

Supporting Your Student

Read *(North and East Africa)*

To best support your student through this section, encourage them to add a compass rose to the map. Ask them to consider how important water is to life and to civilization as they observe the Nile and the seas around this area.

Read *(West, Central, and Southern Africa)*

Adding the compass rose to the second map will help students with the names of the regions. Note that the equator runs through the Congo just like it does in the Amazon. The equator draws moisture from both hemispheres, and this makes huge tropical rain forests possible.

Practice

To best support your student through this section, encourage looking at several maps. To further their learning, ask questions like, "What is the tallest mountain in Africa?," "What are the mountains in the northwest called?," and "Where can you find diamonds?"

Learning Styles

Auditory learners may enjoy listening to a travel podcast about various geographical features in Africa. They may also enjoy listening to different types of music from Africa.

Visual learners may enjoy going on a virtual safari to see the grasslands and the animals that live there. They may also enjoy watching various types of traditional dances from Africa.

Kinesthetic learners may enjoy creating a diorama to depict one of the geographic regions.

Extension Activities

Create a Slide Presentation

Have your student create a slideshow presentation with pictures and information about the geography of Africa. They should include information about the regions, locations of the ancient kingdoms, and notable geographical features.

Create a Travel Brochure

Have your student create a travel brochure for one of the regions of Africa. Have your student include pictures of the physical features that someone would see when traveling to that region as well as any other information that they choose to include. Assist your student in searching for additional information online to add to the brochure along with pictures.

Answer Key

Write *(Based on what you already know about other ancient civilizations, explain why it makes sense that so many early African civilizations arose in North and East Africa.)*

Answers will vary. Possible answer: Your student should note that North and East Africa are near Mesopotamia, Israel, India, Greece, and/or Rome by sea routes.

Practice

Answers will vary. Check your student's map to ensure that they correctly labeled each place on the map.

Show What You Know

1. B
2. C
3. A
4. D
5. E
6. Answers will vary. Possible answer: Africa is broken up into five regions: North, East, West, Central, and Southern. Carthage, Egypt, and Nubia (Cush/Kush) were located in North Africa between the Nile and the Red Sea. Aksum stretched across the border of North and East Africa much like modern day Ethiopia. The Ghana Empire was in West Africa. One unifying feature for all these kingdoms was access to water for agriculture and trade.

Lesson Objectives

By the end of this lesson, your student will be able to:

- identify methods of learning about civilizations that did not have a written language
- identify the role of an African griot in preserving a people's history
- explain how linguistics can be used to track the migration of a people group
- explain how botany can be used to gain information about a people group

Supporting Your Student

Read *(Learning About Ancient Civilizations)*
To best support your student through this section, explain the value of passing down stories from generation to generation. Ask your student if they remember any stories that older family members have told them about their life. Help them to understand the value in history being passed down in this manner by explaining that even though a civilization did not write to record their history, they used other methods to share their history, traditions, and culture.

Read *(Using Linguistics to Track Migration)*
To best support your student through this section, give them familiar examples. Explain names of landmarks, roads, and/or nearby towns that are used because of another culture that existed in that place previously. For example, the culture and language of the French is easily identified in Louisiana and the culture and language of the Spanish is easily identified in Florida and throughout the US southwest.

Read *(Using Botany to Gain Information)*
To best support your student through this section, ask them about the plants and crops that grow near your home. Ask them what others could learn about your culture based on what grows near you. For example, if you live near an apple orchard, people most likely eat lots of fresh apples and your area may be known for its apples or even host an apple festival. Help them to make the connection between what grows well in your area to what people centuries ago would have relied on for a source of food.

Learning Styles

Auditory learners may enjoy recording their personal oral history to play for family members and friends in the future. They may also enjoy listening to traditional African folktales.

Visual learners may enjoy studying maps of migration patterns and colonization in Africa to gain a better understanding of the impact of linguistics on the people living in Africa today.

Kinesthetic learners may enjoy drawing pictures to represent the variety of crops and plants growing in different regions of Africa to gain a better understanding of what the ancient civilizations located in that region grew and harvested as a food source.

Extension Activities

Create a Storyboard

Have your student draw a storyboard to depict an event in history that could be shared by a griot. Your student could draw a war, drought, or marriage ceremony. Have your student caption the storyboard with lyrics that a griot would have sung for that story.

Make a Multimedia Presentation

Have your student conduct research on the languages currently spoken in a region of Africa. They should demonstrate their knowledge of linguistics in a multimedia presentation that explains who has lived in that region in the past based on the languages used in the present day.

Answer Key

Write (Identify and explain the role a griot plays in preserving the history of West Africa.)

Answers will vary. Possible answers: A griot is an oral historian who tells stories of the past. They are responsible for keeping track of all wars, droughts, births, deaths, and marriages in their family or village by memorizing all of this information. They play a vital role in their society as their work keeps the traditions and culture alive through both history and folktales that teach lessons about how to act properly.

Write (How can we use linguistics to track the migration of people groups?)

Answers will vary. Possible answer: One way to track how ancient civilizations migrated is through linguistics. Historians are able to track where different groups migrated based on the versions of languages spoken in those areas today. By studying the linguistic patterns of the people of Africa today, historians are able to tell us which ancient civilizations migrated through those countries centuries ago.

Write (Explain how botany can be used to better understand people groups.)

Answers will vary. Possible answer: Botany is used to help historians better understand a people group based on the plants that lived in that area. By studying plant life in an area where an ancient civilization was living, historians are able to better understand what people ate. Historians can also learn about the agriculture of an area by better understanding what types of plants can thrive in that climate.

Show What You Know

1. Answers will vary. Possible answer: One way to learn about the past is through oral history. For centuries, people have used oral communication to pass down stories about their families, important events, and their culture. These stories have given historians great insight into cultures that were previously a mystery. In West Africa, historians who tell stories of the past are called griots. Griots began telling the stories of the people of the Mali Kingdom in West Africa in the thirteenth century and still share their people's history orally to this day. A griot tells their story to music and is responsible for keeping track of all wars, droughts, births, deaths, and marriages in their family or village by memorizing all of this information. Griots play a vital role in their society, keeping tradition and culture alive as they tell the history of the Mali Kingdom centuries after its fall.

2. Linguistics

3. Botany

4. migration

5. food

Lesson Objectives

By the end of this lesson, your student will be able to:

- describe cultural characteristics of different ancient African people groups
- analyze the effects of the Bantu migration on culture

Supporting Your Student

Read (Cultural Characteristics of Ancient African Peoples)

To best support your student in this section, have them highlight or underline key pieces of information for each of the ancient African people groups in different colors. For example, have them use blue for religious beliefs, yellow for home region, and orange for lifestyle (such as whether the people are nomads, semi-nomads, or settled in villages). Any colors will do as long as they are used consistently. Your student will use the highlighted information in the Practice section.

Read (Effects of the Bantu Migration on Culture)

To support your student in this section, explain to them the difference between a sudden migration caused by war or disaster and a long, drawn out migration. As an example of gradual migration, the US states in the sunbelt have been gaining populations from midwest industrial states over the last 50 years.

Learning Styles

Auditory learners may enjoy listening to oral histories of these ancient groups, found in online videos.

Visual learners may enjoy looking at pictures and maps that depict the culture of the Taureg, Maasai, Mbuti, San, and Khoikhoi peoples.

Kinesthetic learners may enjoy designing an infographic to show their knowledge of the ancient people groups and the locations of their homelands. Your student could include cultural information as well as a map showing the homelands of the various groups.

Extension Activities

Analyze a Song

Help your student find a traditional or contemporary song by an African musician or group. They may need a translation. Have them identify what the singer values by the content of the song, and discuss with them why this value is important to the singer and his/her nation.

Guess That Group

Play a game with your student where they give you clues about a people group or their location and you have to guess which group your student is describing.

Answer Key

Write *(Analyze the ways the Bantu migration changed other cultures in Africa.)*
Answers will vary. Possible answers: Key details include the Bantu speakers spread agriculture and technology (metal-working).

Practice

Culture	Nomad, Semi-nomad, or Settled	Religion	Geographical Region
Southern Tuareg	Semi-nomad	Muslim	North Africa
Northern Tuareg	Nomad	Muslim	North Africa
Maasai	Semi-nomad	Monotheistic	East Africa
Mbuti	Nomad	Forest god	Central Africa
San	Nomad	Creator god	Southern Africa
Khoikhoi	Settled	Christian	Southern Africa
Xhosa	Settled	Christian	Southern Africa

Show What You Know

1. B
2. D
3. C
4. E
5. A
6. Central
7. West
8. San People
9. Maasai

Lesson Objectives

By the end of this lesson, your student will be able to:

- describe Aksum's culture, language, and resources
- identify what likely influenced Ezana's spiritual conversion and how it influenced his kingdom
- describe ancient African legends and how they were based on the lives of real people

Supporting Your Student

Read (The Kingdom of Aksum)

To best support your student through this section, help them locate the kingdom of Aksum on a map. The kingdom's location included fertile land and was an advantageous location for trade. Once your student understands the location of Aksum, they will be able to see how the Aksumites could control trade in the Red Sea.

Read (King Ezana)

To best support your student through this section, discuss what conversion means with your student. King Ezana's conversion parallels that of Emperor Constantine. When the leader converts, everyone converts. Ask your student to compare the two events.

Read (Ancient African Legends)

To best support your student through this section, help them think of legends familiar to them. Ask them what stories they have heard about historical figures that might not be entirely based on facts. King Arthur and the search for the Holy Grail is a good example. Although not as lighthearted and friendly as some folktales, legends also try to help people understand difficult concepts like virtues, hope, death, and keeping important memories. By helping your student recall legends with which they are already familiar, they will have a better understanding of the concept of legends and their role in the study of ancient Africa.

Learning Styles

Auditory learners may enjoy listening to African legends found on the internet.

Visual learners may enjoy taking a virtual tour or watching a video of modern-day Ethiopia to see the Aksumite ruins that still exist today. You can find a virtual tour or video by searching online.

Kinesthetic learners may enjoy creating an obelisk out of modeling clay.

Extension Activities

Create a Legend for the Queen of Sheba

Many writers have imagined stories about the Queen of Sheba. She reigned in a time and place where most leaders were men. She controlled fabulous wealth. The Queen of Sheba is supposed to be the mother of a dynasty that lasted nearly 3,000 years. Have your student create their own legend about this fabulous historical figure.

Write a Letter

Have your student write a letter from King Ezana to his former tutor, Frumentius, explaining how his life and the lives of his people changed after he converted to Christianity. Your student should write in first person, as if they are King Ezana, and give specific examples of what their life is like following conversion.

Answer Key

Write *(What did trade bring to Aksum?)*
Answers will vary. Possible answers: Trade brought new ideas including architecture. Trade brought gold, jewels, ivory, and wealth.

Write *(How did King Ezana's conversion to Christianity impact the Kingdom of Aksum?)*
Answers will vary. Possible answers: The Kingdom of Aksum converted to Christianity, and the coins featured images of crosses and the words the Father, the Son, and the Holy Spirit.

Write *(What is a legend? Who are African legends based on?)*
A legend is a story that is sometimes believed to be historically true but cannot be proven to be based on fact. Legends of Africa focus on leaders from across the continent. Legends are different from folktales or mythology because they focus on a specific (probably) real person.

Show What You Know
1. False
2. True
3. False
4. True
5. True
6. False
7. True
8. Answers will vary. Possible answer: Obelisks are memorials like tombstones. They were raised to commemorate great victories.

Lesson Objectives

By the end of this lesson, your student will be able to:

- identify the sources of the Ghana Empire's wealth
- describe the changes that led to the Ghana Empire's expansion

Supporting Your Student

Read (The Ghana Empire)

To best support your student through this section, discuss taxes with them. Help them to understand how the kings made money from items leaving and entering the country through taxation. Also, you might remind your student about the terms *scarcity* and *abundance*, which have been introduced several times before this lesson. Salt was scarce on the coast of West Africa, where gold and ivory were abundant and vice versa. Trade begins when someone has something that someone else wants or needs.

Read (Change and Growth)

To best support your student through this section, discuss how the spread of Islam in the 600s affected the world economy by creating new trade networks.

Read (Why Does the Ghana Empire Matter?)

To best support your student through this section, encourage your student to consider how modern cities exist in places that are very different from the earliest cities, as with Koumbi Saleh. Texas could serve as an example. Of the major cities in Texas, only Houston has access to shipping by water. Austin, Dallas/Fort Worth, San Antonio, Amarillo, El Paso, Lubbock, and Abilene all thrive because of alternate methods to move trade goods besides boats. There may be other places closer to your area that could serve as examples.

Learning Styles

Auditory learners may enjoy listening to oral histories and folktales about the people of West Africa and determining the civilization of origin for each story.

Visual learners may enjoy watching videos about life in the desert and how people and animals adapt to this extreme climate.

Kinesthetic learners may enjoy creating a play or pantomime that shows how trade works. West Africa is the home to many languages, and sometimes traders had to trade without using any common language.

Extension Activities

Create a Movie

Have your student create a movie to compare and contrast ancient Ghana and modern-day Ghana. Have your student include images, a map, and a voice-over to share their understanding of these two people groups.

Create a Map

Have your student create a map with text and images to depict trade in West Africa and how it made ancient Ghana wealthy. Have your student include what entered the country and what exited, as well as the taxation of those items.

LESSON 69
Ancient Ghana

Answer Key

Write *(How did Islam affect the Ghana Empire's economy?)*
Answers will vary. Possible answers: The growth of Islam expanded trade networks from North Africa to new areas. The increased number of connections expanded the number of people who could access the gold and ivory of West Africa.

Online Connection
Answers will vary. Possible answer: Prior to refrigeration, preserving meat required large quantities of salt. Meat could be packed in salt to keep fresh, or salt could be used to dry meat into jerky.

Show What You Know
1. Atlantic
2. Sahara
3. alluvial
4. Muslims
5. desert
6. salt
7. taxes
8. copper
9. expanded
10. Koumbi Saleh
11. Answers will vary. Possible answers: Trade made the empire of Ghana very wealthy. Ghana traded items such as gold and ivory to traders from North Africa who paid for things in salt. The kings of Ghana taxed anything entering or leaving the Ghana Empire. In addition, the kings of Ghana controlled the gold market by preventing anyone other than themselves from owning, selling, or trading gold.

Lesson Objectives

By the end of this lesson, your student will be able to:

- locate ancient Mali and the modern country of Mali on a map
- identify famous rulers of Mali and describe their accomplishments
- describe the culture of ancient Mali

Supporting Your Student

Explore

You can support your student by asking them questions about fairness. The ideas of fairness, competition, and self-esteem are important to middle school students.

Read (Sundiata)

You can support your student by pointing out that the moral code of Islam can be reduced to the Five Pillars of Islam: (1) belief that there is one God; (2) prayer (devout Muslims stop to pray five times a day); (3) alms (it is important to give to the poor); (4) fasting (at certain times, Muslims fast to show God their piety); and (5) Hajj (taking a pilgrimage journey to Mecca). Alms and the Hajj may explain why Mansa Musa gave away all the gold he brought on his journey to Mecca.

Read (Mali Culture)

Discuss the importance of education in a successful culture with your student.

Learning Styles

Auditory learners may enjoy finding an online lesson about the Mali Empire and listening to the explanations. They may also enjoy listening to recordings of a Muslim call to prayer.

Visual learners may enjoy creating a slideshow of Mali culture from online sources.

Kinesthetic learners may enjoy a building project. For example, your student might create a Mali-style building using toothpicks or craft sticks and homemade playdough. Your student can make their own playdough from food coloring, flour, salt and vegetable oil.

Extension Activity

Racing in the Sahara

Have your student prepare a report about the Paris-Dakar Rally. The race traditionally runs through North Africa. Drivers choose to ride motorcycles or drive specially modified cars or trucks.

Answer Key

Write *(Describe the cultural advances to Mali culture during Mansa Musa's rule.)*
Answers will vary. Possible answers: religious tolerance, wood-fired bricks, and education

Show What You Know

1. Mali
2. Mansa Musa
3. salt
4. gold
5. mosque
6. Answers will vary. Possible answer: One change could be identified as technology (firing bricks) or architecture (taller, stronger buildings). Another change could be education (or scholarship). The third change could be religious tolerance, which was a hallmark of early Islam.

Ancient Songhai Civilization

Lesson Objectives

By the end of this lesson, your student will be able to:

- find ancient Songhai on a map
- identify the most significant ruler of Songhai and his accomplishments
- trace the major events that led to the rise and fall of the empires of Mali and Songhai

Supporting Your Student

Explore

You can support your student by helping them understand a vacuum as a metaphor.

Read (Askia the Great)

You can support your student by helping them focus on the topic. In this case, Askia the Great was the only Songhai ruler to last very long. After his reign, a series of kings fought over the throne and the wealth it represented.

Read (Rise and Fall of Empires)

You can support your student to understand that empires take a long time to grow but fall relatively quickly. The fall of an empire is often caused by greed.

Learning Styles

Auditory learners may enjoy finding an online lesson about the Songhai Empire and listening to the explanations.

Visual learners may enjoy creating a visual journal about their reading.

Kinesthetic learners may enjoy acting out one or more of the events described.

Extension Activities

Berbers

Have your student look up information and pictures of the Berber tribes known as Riffians and Kabyle. These North African tribes have many members who are blond and/or have blue or green eyes. Have your student make a slideshow explaining how these European traits entered the African family tree.

Adventure in Morocco

Have your student find pictures or a video of a souk (marketplace) in Morocco. Then challenge them to write a story about a day shopping in a souk.

Answer Key

Write *(Neither the Mali Empire nor the Songhai Empire lasted as long as the Ghana Empire. Why do you think the second two empires did not last as long?)*

Answers will vary. Possible answer: The second two empires did not last as long because of greed. Greed is a common factor in the fall of empires throughout history.

Practice

Answers will vary. Possible answers:

Ghana: rise of Islam

Mali: education and architecture

Songhai: converted nation to Islam

All: salt, gold, and taxes

Show What You Know

1. B
2. D
3. B
4. Answers will vary. Possible answers: The Ghana Empire was most successful because it lasted longest. The Mali Empire was most successful because it enriched the culture with education and stronger buildings. The Songhai Empire was strongest because they had a standing army.

Lesson Objectives

By the end of this lesson, your student will be able to:

- define how the law of supply and demand affects prices in an economy
- describe the economies of Ancient West African civilizations

Supporting Your Student

Explore

You can support your student by helping them understand the difference between ores and alloys. Rocks containing metals are called ores. Ores may contain several metals. For example, calaverite ore found in Cripple Creek, Colorado, is a mineral that contains large amounts of both gold and silver. The metals must be separated chemically in a process called refining. Alloys are created by intentionally mixing metals. Pure silver is so soft it is useless for making coins or jewelry. It must be mixed with other metals to make it useful. For example, sterling silver is 92.5 percent silver and 7.5 percent something else (usually copper). While pure gold is also softer than gold alloys, it is usable in its pure form. Furthermore, gold retains its luster longer than silver.

Read *(Value and Need)*

You can help your student understand the economics of the ancient world with the word *value* rather than *price*. Newspapers and economists focus on prices instead of value in today's world because we use currency to value everything, but in the ancient world things were different. Bartering was more common so value was always negotiable. You could not just trade a camel for 10 bags of rice. A young, strong camel could be worth 10 bags of rice, but an old camel might only be worth two bags of rice. We also use value today to determine what to buy. Some will pay more for an organically farmed head of lettuce because they consider it healthier than lettuce exposed to bug sprays.

Read *(Supply and Demand)*

You can help your student understand supply and demand in various ways from your own experience. To demonstrate value in supply and demand, hide a sample of your student's favorite snack and barter it for chores or money. Then discuss the results with your student.

Learning Styles

Auditory learners may enjoy listening to podcasts about economics.

Visual learners may enjoy creating a comic strip about trade.

Kinesthetic learners may enjoy playing a trading game or bartering with someone else for goods they value.

Extension Activities

Collectables

Have your student choose a collectable item (i.e., art, coins, stamps, comics, Pokémon cards) and research the prices paid at auction for rare items. If possible, have them research how the price has changed over time. Have your student explain why the item is rare and why collectors value the object.

Supply and Demand

Have your student read about the oil crisis of 1979. Was there a change in supply or demand? What happened to the price of oil in the United States? What happened to gasoline prices? Have your student explain how the change in price affected the whole US economy. Have your student show you what they learned in a visual presentation.

Answer Key

Write *(Describe the difference between need and value.)*
Answers will vary. Possible answer: A need is something you must have to survive (i.e., food, water, shelter, security). Value is how much you will trade for a need or desire.

Write *(Describe how supply and demand affected you when you wanted something and had trouble getting it.)*
Answers will vary. Possible answer: A student may remember having to work extra hard to earn a reward. Another scenario may involve being patient or impatient waiting for something to arrive or happen.

Show What You Know

1. supply
2. consumer
3. economy
4. need
5. value
6. demand
7. Answers will vary. Possible answer: Revenue from taxing gold, salt, and trade decreased because the Portuguese traders bypassed the interior land routes that had existed for centuries.

Ancient Mwene Mutapa and Ancient Shona

Lesson Objectives

By the end of this lesson, your student will be able to:

- locate ancient Mwene Mutapa and the modern country of Zimbabwe on a map
- identify features of buildings of Great Zimbabwe

Supporting Your Student

Explore

You can support your student by encouraging them to question easy assumptions gathered from popular movies, television, or books. Great fiction authors use enough truth in their creations that the stories seem to come alive. Likewise, most legends begin with real people but then exaggerate the plot to make a point. The Virginia Museum of History and Culture has a history lesson online about the real John Henry that helps untangle one legend from reality.

Read (From Migration to Empire)

You can support your student by helping them understand that the Bantu migration was gradual, probably village by village. Their superior metal-working technology made them more efficient farmers than others and better able to make weapons to guard their herds or seize good land from their neighbors. Their language also evolved as they migrated from their original home just as the English language has changed since the time of Chaucer to now.

Read (Great Stone Houses)

You can support your student by showing them pictures of modern-day Scottish crofts. A croft is a farm or compound, and many will seem nearly identical to the construction of the stone buildings of Great Zimbabwe.

Learning Styles

Auditory learners may enjoy listening to traditional Bantu singers from South Africa.

Visual learners may enjoy creating sketches of Great Zimbabwe or discovering the sites along the Limpopo River or the Zambezi River.

Kinesthetic learners may enjoy recreating the buildings of Great Zimbabwe.

Extension Activities

Dr. Livingstone

Have your student research and prepare a report on Dr. David Livingstone. Dr. Livingstone was a Scottish missionary who traveled a great deal through southern Africa, including the area described in this lesson. He is the one who gave Victoria Falls its current name. Have your student also research the indengious name of the falls.

Nyami Nyami

Have your student prepare an oral report or retell the legends of Nyami Nyami, the Zambezi River God of the Tonga people. Nyami Nyami is said to live in Lake Kariba and is very angry about the dam that was built on the river.

Answer Key

Write *(Can you think of another ancient structure from around the world that resembles these ruins? How are these structures similar?)*
Answers will vary widely based on your student's experiences. Castles, farmhouses, walls, or anything else made from stacked stones is appropriate.

Practice
Answers will vary. Since scholars often debate about the borders of these ancient kingdoms, your student's drawings do not have to be exact. However, see the map below for general locations of the ancient kingdoms on a map.

Show What You Know
1. D
2. A
3. B
4. A
5. A
6. B
7. Answers will vary. Possible answers: Both cultures traded gold. Both cultures had an agricultural base. Ghana developed a tax system, but Mwene Mutapa did not.

Lesson Objectives

By the end of this lesson, your student will be able to:

- label places on a map of Africa
- identify common features of the coastal cities in Africa
- identify how traders and explorers influenced Africa and whether the results were positive or negative

Supporting Your Student

Explore

You can support your student by helping them envision or imagine what it was like to risk one's life to discover something new over the horizon. Encourage role playing or drawing to ignite their imagination. Old films about sea travel from the golden era of Hollywood might also aid the visualization.

Read (A Time Before Maps)

To support your student, explore different kinds of online coastal maps together. A satellite map of the Caribbean can help your student explore reefs and sandbars that make sailing difficult. You can also point out on the Caribbean map where the Gulf Stream current has cut a groove between Florida and the Bahamas.

Read (The Slave Trade)

You can support your student by taking time to listen and by being prepared to share your own feelings about the subject. Research shows that children begin to develop their own sense of morality beginning around age eight. Moral development continues gradually through the teens and twenties. Your student may have questions about justice and other complicated moral issues.

Learning Styles

Auditory learners may enjoy an audiobook about adventures on the high seas.

Visual learners may enjoy watching an old movie about life on a sailing vessel.

Kinesthetic learners may enjoy role-playing the life of a sailor aboard an old ship.

Extension Activities

Scurvy

Have your student prepare a quick oral report about the disease called scurvy. You might have them answer questions such as, "How did it affect sailors during the Age of Exploration?," "What is the cause of scurvy?," and "What is the cure for scurvy?"

Seychelles

Have your student prepare a travel brochure for the Seychelles Islands, one of the world's smallest countries. They should include at least five interesting facts that might convince someone to visit the islands.

Answer Key

Write

Answers will vary. Ensure your student has supported their answer with an explanation.

Practice

Show What You Know

1. 3

2. 2

3. 4

4. 1

5. 5

6. True

7. False

8. Answers will vary. Possible answer: The new supply of gold and silver from the New World caused the value of gold to decrease, creating a shift from the value of gold to the value of slaves for labor.

Ancient African Cultural Contributions

Lesson Objectives

By the end of this lesson, your student will be able to:

- examine the historical route and significance of the art of fabric dyeing to African culture and trade
- recognize ancient African cultural contributions

Supporting Your Student

Explore

To support your student in understanding cultural influences, point out local ethnic influences. For example, Lindsborg, Kansas, was settled by Swedes. You can see the influence of German people in Mexico City in their dairy, brewing, and carpentry industries. Pennsylvania contains many Welsh place names such as Bryn Mawr. Towns from Phillips, Wisconsin, down to West Texas and all of the states in between hold annual Czech festivals.

Read (Fiber Arts)

To help your student understand the importance of fiber art traditions in cultures, have them research traditional clothing from their own cultural heritage to see the wide variety of colors, styles, and materials.

Read (Musical Contributions)

To support your student understanding beats, have them clap out a beat of four claps with no stress while counting each beat. Have them repeat this several times. Then have them clap the beat stressing the first beat: ONE-two-three-four. This is a standard beat in European music, where the strongest emphasis is on the downbeat, or first beat. Now, have your student stress the second beat: one-TWO-three-four. This is the backbeat mentioned in the reading. The musician should feel the downbeat but highlight the backbeat.

Learning Styles

Auditory learners may enjoy comparing traditional African music to contemporary pop music to find similarities.

Visual learners may enjoy videos about African cloth and basket weaving traditions.

Kinesthetic learners may enjoy building a simple loom and weaving a loose piece of fabric.

Extension Activities

Fashion!

Have your student prepare a report on African prints used in the fashion industry. Have them share their report with you in the form of a slideshow, fashion show, or written report with illustrations.

Medicine

Have your student research medicines and medical treatments that originated in Africa. Have them share their findings with you, making sure they explain what the medicines are for and how the treatments are used today.

Ancient African Cultural Contributions

Answer Key

Write *(Where do cloth fibers come from?)*

Answers will vary. Possible answer: Cloth fibers come from plant sources (i.e, cotton plants, flax, palm, or bark) and animal hair sources (i.e., wool from goats or camels). Although not mentioned, leather is an intuitive answer that may be accepted.

Practice

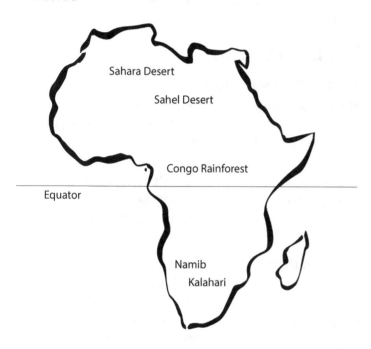

Show What You Know

1. True
2. False
3. False
4. True
5. False
6. True
7. Answers will vary. Your student may concentrate on the African cultural contributions of fiber arts and music due to the context of the lesson. Your student may choose to offer cultural gifts from their own family or regional experiences. They should clearly name cultural contributions and provide examples in their writing.

Lesson Objectives

In this lesson, your student will review the following big ideas from Chapter 10.

- Rivers and oceans are key to the development of civilizations in Africa. (Lesson 65)
- Oral history, linguistics, and botany provide clues to understanding the past. (Lesson 66)
- The Bantu Migration spread Iron Age technology across Sub Saharan Africa. (Lesson 67)
- Ancient Aksum was an early stronghold of Christianity in Africa. (Lesson 68)
- Taxing the gold and salt trade was fundamental to ancient Ghana's success. (Lesson 69)
- Ancient Mali created a monopoly by claiming both the gold and salt sources. (Lesson 70)
- Ancient Songhai was defeated by European weapons. (Lesson 71)
- Exporting natural resources like gold, silver, and copper fed ancient African economies. (Lesson 72)
- Mwene Mutapa's architectural achievements showed sophisticated technology. (Lesson 73)
- Portuguese explorers broke the Arab monopoly on gold and slaves. (Lesson 74)
- Ancient Africa's rich cultural contributions continue to grace the world. (Lesson 75)

Supporting Your Student

Practice (Vocabulary)
Have your student make flash cards. Your student may also enjoy making songs out of the words to remember them.

Practice (Chronological Order)
Encourage your student to write each empire on a sticky note or index card. They can then move the events into different orders and discuss the reason for each placement until they understand the correct order.

Learning Styles

Auditory learners may enjoy rehearsing their answers orally with a recording device to capture their ideas before writing.

Visual learners may enjoy charting answers in graphic organizers before writing.

Kinesthetic learners may enjoy creating and using flash cards with different facts they learned about Africa.

Extension Activities

Poster Presentation
Have your student create a poster containing information about life in one of the ancient kingdoms. Ask them to include images of art and architecture, details about the locations, and information about the economics of ancient Africa. After they have created their poster, have them present the information to you as though they are teaching you about ancient Africa.

Study Guide
Have your student create a study guide before their assessment. Ask them to include key vocabulary, maps, and connections between the lessons. After they have created their study guide, have them explain how they will use it to prepare for the assessment.

Answer Key

Write *(Identify one major change from the beginning of the Ghana Empire to the end of the Songhai Empire.)*
Answers will vary. Possible answers: Each empire was larger than the previous one. Each empire lasted a shorter time than the previous one. Mali and Songhai had monopolies on the entire gold and salt trade but Ghana did not.

Write *(Identify two ways Mwene Mutapa was similar to the West African empires.)*
Answers will vary. Possible answers: similar levels of technology (iron work/agriculture), the gold trade

Practice *(Vocabulary)*
Answers will vary. Possible answers:

1. a scientist that studies culture
2. a person who buys goods or services for personal use
3. a type of African musician who tells stories with songs
4. a cloth woven in thin strips
5. a place a Muslim person worships
6. the transition zone between the Sahara and the rain forest
7. a name that means stone house

Practice *(Chronological Order)*
2, 1, 4, 6, 3, 5

Write *(What were the reasons for the shift from the gold trade to the slave trade in the 1500s?)*
Answers will vary. Possible answers: The reasons are gold from the New World increased supply, which decreased the value of gold, and the need for labor in the New World made slaves more valuable.

Practice *(Regions)*
1. Southern Africa, East Africa
2. East Africa
3. West Africa
4. West Africa
5. West Africa
6. North Africa

Quick Review

Refer to the statement your student circled in the Show What You Know section to self-assess their knowledge of the chapter concepts. Then to assist in determining if your student is ready to take the assessment, consider:

- Having your student tell you the names of each region in Africa (north, west, east, central, and southern).
- Having your student describe the natural resources Africa has, such as gold.
- Having your student explain that African civilization spread from the Nile Valley to other parts of Africa and that Bantu migration helped spread technology across Sub-Saharan Africa.
- Having your student explain why the West African empires depended on trade (salt for gold) and taxation.
- Having your student explain that Arab (Muslim) traders had a monopoly of the gold and other goods from African for many years.
- Having your student describe how the slave trade spread African people to the Americas and Caribbean.

Chapter Assessment

Circle the correct answer.

1. True or False   Africa is divided into four geographical regions: Sahara, Nile, Sahel, and mountains.

2. True or False   Africa is divided into five geographical regions: Sahara, Sahel, Great Rift, Southern Savanna, and Congo Rainforest.

3. True or False   The Sahara is in the Northern Hemisphere.

4. True or False   Aksum was home to the first civilization in Africa.

5. True or False   Madagascar was first settled by people for Malaysia.

6. True or False   The Silk Road had a water route through the Red Sea.

7. True or False   Obelisks are mythological creatures.

8. Aksum's king introduced _____ to his people.
   A. higher education
   B. Christianity
   C. Islam
   D. stone houses

9. Ancient Mali introduced _____ to West Africa.
   A. higher education
   B. Christianity
   C. Islam
   D. stone houses

10. The Shona people were part of the _____.
    A. spread of Islam
    B. Bantu influence
    C. Bantu migration
    D. Bantu uprising

11. The first Europeans to sail around Africa to India were the _____.
    A. Dutch
    B. Italians
    C. Spanish
    D. Portuguese

12. The term Mwene Mutapa refers to _____.
    A. both a king and an empire
    B. stone houses
    C. a North African empire
    D. an early Christian missionary

13. A camel can carry _____.
    A. up to 300 grams
    B. up to 300 pounds
    C. up to 300 kilos
    D. up to one ton

14. Ge'ez script was the writing system of _____.
    A. Egypt
    B. Mwene Mutapa
    C. Aksum
    D. Empire of Ghana

Discover! SOCIAL STUDIES • GRADE 6 • CHAPTER 10 ASSESSMENT

219

Use the words from the Word Bank to complete the sentences.

Word Bank: salt   camels   Sahel   Islam
stone house   savanna   Nile

15. Zimbabwe means _____.

16. Ancient Egypt grew along the
_____ River.

17. The _____ is the transition zone between the Sahara and the Congo rainforest.

18. Another name for an African grassland is
_____.

19. _____ are sometimes called the ships of the desert.

20. In West Africa, _____ was once worth its weight in gold.

21. In the 600s, the religion called
_____ swept across North Africa.

Answer the following question in complete sentences.

22. How did the ancient Ghana Empire make money from trade?

....

....

....

....

Chapter Assessment Answer Key

1. False
2. False
3. True
4. False
5. True
6. True
7. False
8. B
9. A
10. C
11. D
12. A
13. B
14. C
15. stone house
16. Nile
17. Sahel
18. savanna
19. Camels
20. salt
21. Islam
22. Answers will vary. Possible answer: The ancient Ghana Empire made money from taxes, such as on gold, salt, copper, and ivory.

Discover! SOCIAL STUDIES • GRADE 6 • CHAPTER 10 ASSESSMENT

221

Alternative Assessment

Project: Editorial

An editorial is an article or piece of writing similar to a newspaper column that offers opinions and personal perspectives. For this project, have your student write an editorial that includes their opinions or perspectives on an issue presented in the chapter. They may write their editorial in a way similar to a newspaper column.

Project Requirements:

The project should include:

- a headline
- a focused theme and opinion
- an alternative view to the opinion (such as, "While those who disagree with me might say...")
- a call to action for the reader to solve the problem

Alternative Assessment Rubric

Use the following rubric to grade your student's assessment.

	4	3	2	1	Points
Creativity and Organization	The editorial presents the opinion with supportive facts and presents the opposing opinion clearly.	The editorial presents the opinion with weak facts but presents the opposing opinion clearly.	The editorial presents the opinion with no facts and does not present the opposing opinion.	The editorial does not present the opinion or the opposing opinion.	
Instruction	The editorial provides a clear and strong call to action along with the opinion.	The editorial provides a weak but clear call to action along with the opinion.	The editorial provides a weak and unclear call to action along with the opinion.	The editorial provides no call to action with no opinion.	
Practice	The editorial makes clear and repetitive connections to the chapter and includes all the required elements.	The editorial is related to the chapter but does not include all required elements.	The editorial makes one or two references to the chapter but does not include all required elements.	The editorial is unrelated to the chapter and does not include all required elements.	
Presentation	The editorial contains no grammar issues and advanced vocabulary.	The editorial contains a few grammar mistakes and age-appropriate vocabulary.	The editorial contains several grammar mistakes and age-appropriate vocabulary.	The editorial contains a distracting number of grammar mistakes and overly simplified vocabulary.	

Total Points _____/16

Average _____